# HAMLET
## FATHER AND SON

*Oxford University Press, Ely House, London W. 1*

GLASGOW   NEW YORK   TORONTO   MELBOURNE   WELLINGTON
CAPE TOWN   SALISBURY   IBADAN   NAIROBI   LUSAKA   ADDIS ABABA
BOMBAY   CALCUTTA   MADRAS   KARACHI   LAHORE   DACCA
KUALA LUMPUR   HONG KONG   TOKYO

# HAMLET
## FATHER AND SON

---

*The Lord Northcliffe Lectures*
*University College, London*
*1953*

BY

PETER ALEXANDER

OXFORD
AT THE CLARENDON PRESS

17689

Τοῦ γὰρ ἀθανάτου ἐρῶσιν

FIRST PUBLISHED 1955
REPRINTED LITHOGRAPHICALLY IN GREAT BRITAIN
AT THE UNIVERSITY PRESS, OXFORD
FROM SHEETS OF THE FIRST EDITION
1963, 1967

# PREFACE

IN accepting the invitation to deliver the Lord Northcliffe lectures, with which the Provost and Governing Body of University College, London, had honoured me, I expressed my thanks for what was to me a specially gracious gesture, for the first lecturer on this foundation was my predecessor at Glasgow, William Macneile Dixon. My next thought was to find a topic that would allow me, in the conditions prescribed by the deed of gift, to develop some aspect of a subject that Macneile Dixon himself had regarded as central in the study of literature.

Such a topic seemed provided me by Sir Laurence Olivier's film version of *Hamlet*. A film that some 20 million spectators have at several times applauded would set the discussion on the broader lines indicated by the donors, Viscount Rothermere and Lord Harmsworth, of this memorial to their brother; while a film that begins by offering the spectators a definite idea, in the form of a Prologue, of the significance of this play challenges comment from students of Shakespeare. For the challenge is bold and unequivocal. We are told we are about to see the tragedy of a man who could not make up his mind; and the voice of the Prologue offers us as Shakespeare's own comment on the hero's infirmity of purpose the lines Hamlet himself speaks on the battlements:

> So, oft it chances in particular men
> That, for some vicious mole of nature in them,
> As in their birth, wherein they are not guilty,
> Since nature cannot choose his origin;
> By the o'ergrowth of some complexion,
> Oft breaking down the pales and forts of reason;
> Or by some habit that too much o'er-leavens
> The form of plausive manners—that these men,
> Carrying, I say, the stamp of one defect,
> Being nature's livery or fortune's star,
> His virtues else, be they as pure as grace,
> As infinite as man may undergo,
> Shall in the general censure take corruption
> From that particular fault.

Mr. Alan Dent, who co-operated in the production of the film, was for a time a pupil of Macneile Dixon; the pupil, however, in allowing without protest such a Prologue to *Hamlet* had forgotten or rejected his master's teaching. It seemed therefore not inappropriate for another of Macneile Dixon's pupils to submit the notion of tragedy adopted by the film-producer to examination, and to cast the lectures into the form of a friendly controversy. On one side the arguments and authorities

that Mr. Alan Dent might cite for his idea, on the
other the reasons why these arguments and authorities do not justify the weight he has placed on them,
were to be brought forward and submitted to the
scrutiny of the audience. Deliberate unfairness or
any tampering with the witnesses would, it was
hoped, be prevented by so open a procedure.

As my intention is not to offer dogmatic instruction but rather to appeal to those who are
interested in the subject, as I did to the listeners,
to look first upon this picture and then on this, I
have retained in print the informality of the spoken
word and submit the argument in its original form
to the judgement of the reader.

For the kindness and hospitality with which the
Provost, Professor Sutherland, and members of his
staff, entertained me during my visits to London;
and for the unfailing good humour and indulgence
of my audience, I now offer my very grateful thanks.

P.A.

# CONTENTS

I. FROM SCHOOL IN WITTENBERG    1

II. THE SUBSTANCE OF TRAGEDY    40

III. THE HEROIC TRADITION    79

IV. THE UNION OF OPPOSITES    115

V. THE COMPLETE MAN    151

# I

## FROM SCHOOL IN WITTENBERG

'RAW material for acting' is one of Granville-Barker's less happy definitions of a play by Shakespeare. The great producer was indeed scoring a point, underlining a truth for the instruction of those made insensitive, by too much study of academic criticism shall we say, to the vital part in the plays contributed by Shakespeare's technical mastery in his *métier*; but the remark is so far from being the whole truth that it leads, if the deliberate exaggeration is not allowed for, to untenable conclusions. We might as fairly say that Beethoven's symphonies are raw material for fiddlers and drummers; the composer was like Shakespeare a great technician, yet such a description of his highly organized musical forms would be felt to be inadequate. The point of view to which Granville-Barker would, for his purpose, take us must not make us forget what we may have seen from even more commanding ground—the carefully organized and unified structure of Shakespeare's tragedies; nor must Granville-Barker's observations from his chosen platform persuade us to accept his assertion.

where his original exaggeration passes into distortion, that

The play as it leaves Shakespeare's hands is not a finished product, only its performance makes it that;

or his even more fantastic suggestion that the text of a play is a libretto waiting to be scored by the actor.

Here you may say we have come at too early a stage in our inquiry on one of those philosophical questions that stand in all their entanglements before most critical positions. Is a novel, for instance, an unfinished product till you read it? Is the music of the masters waiting for us to give it the finishing touches? Is a piece of sculpture incomplete till the public is pleased to look it over? To those of Berkeley's way of thinking the sculpture need present no problem, for, like the tree that

> Continues to be
> When there's no one about in the Quad,

it is observed in our absence, the follower of Berkeley has reminded us, by God. But the novel and particularly the music, having perhaps a more metaphysical existence than statuary, raise subsidiary questions that you cannot stay to hear answered, especially as the whole problem admits of a much simpler if less frontal approach.

Some time ago Pablo Casals gave an interview to

a representative of the British Broadcasting Corporation. Inevitably the talk turned for part of the time on Bach, for Casals is, as you know, the first 'cellist who has been able to demonstrate that Bach's 'cello suites can be adequately performed on the instrument they were written for. A brief mention of some of the technical difficulties prompted the interviewer to ask: 'What were performers in Bach's own day able to do about these difficulties? Had Bach no thought about their limitations?' And the answer seems to me most instructive: 'Bach did not care about what the performers could do. He had something to say and said it, and put it in a drawer.' Suppose now we imagine ourselves opening that drawer: what do we take out? Is it an unfinished product that we are going to complete, or is it a highly organized and finished creation that will reveal its perfection only to long and devoted study?

Granville-Barker's remark was suggested to him by his study of *Hamlet*, but it is clear from Hamlet's words to the players how Shakespeare regarded the actor. It was the actor's first duty to attend to the necessary questions of the play, and to deliver the author's lines with sense and sensibility. Hamlet's words were originally spoken on the stage by Burbage, the acknowledged master of his art, to a group of fellow actors who, as a company, can hardly have had superiors in their calling. After Shakespeare's death his colleagues Heminge and Condell in setting forth their friend's dramatic pieces in the First Folio observe that only those readers who dd not understand Shakespeare's words will fail to enjoy him— and such readers they refer to the guidance of Shakespeare's friends, the actors. The actor is to Heminge and Condell, as he was to Shakespeare, the interpreter.

However complicated then the relation of dramatist and actor, composer and executant, it will be sufficient for the present to say that the actress playing the part of Ophelia is no more like Mozart working on Da Ponte's libretto than is the singer studying the part of Susanna in *Figaro*. The comparison formulated by Granville-Barker is absurd if taken without the most liberal qualification. The actor is not like a composer; at his best he is like Casals playing Bach; and Casals prides himself on playing Bach, not on what he likes to make of Bach. There is a compulsion, a service that is inescapable. There are occasions, no doubt, when it is proper to dwell on the executant's contribution to a performance; in the discussion that follows, however, it will be irrelevant to say that a performance or rendering is popular or good theatre or good box-office, or good what you will, if it is not good Shakespeare.

Shakespeare has in *Hamlet* disclosed his own interest and that of his company in the proper performance of the plays; and historians of the drama have now made us feel how superior Elizabethan and Jacobean productions of these plays must have been to what passed on the later stage till comparatively recent times for Shakespeare. The old cry about the crudity and barbarity of Shakespeare's theatre has given place to a desire to get back to the Elizabethan stage. Here, however, the imitation of mere externals will not achieve our purpose. Today the audible form in which we hear the works of the great classical composers is different from that of their own time. There is a close connexion between acoustical perception and musical experience, but it is not mechanical. No mechanical reproduction of Elizabethan conditions, even if it were possible (and it is impossible, since the Elizabethan accent and intonation are no longer practicable on our stage), would be sufficient. There is, however, no need to despair. Casals plays Bach better than the 'cellists of Bach's own day did; it is perhaps to strain the analogy to hope we can perform Shakespeare better than the King's men with the dramatist himself there to help them; we can, however, divest ourselves of the presumption that has for so many years seemed the inevitable habit of the performers and critics of Shakespeare.

To be fair to most modern productions of Shakespeare one ought to have some idea of what actors were doing to Shakespeare not long after his death and particularly from the Restoration reopening of the theatres. It was not that the theatre lacked good actors—Garrick was surely amongst the best of those that have graced the English stage—but some of the versions Garrick played in, above all his own adaptation of *Hamlet*, must be judged almost as bad, on the standard we are using, as anything of this kind before or since. From the faults that come from supposing you are blest with a sureness of taste and a genius for the stage that were beyond the comprehension of a provincial like Shakespeare we are gradually freeing ourselves. When we review the abominable style in which it was once fashionable to rewrite Shakespeare, the modern actor may indeed say like the player in *Hamlet*:

I hope we have reformed that indifferently with us.

And we can only urge him to reform it altogether.

To be fair on the other hand to the old actors we have to remember that an actor is more at what we may call the mercy of the public than any other artist. With the Restoration there were changes both in the audience that frequented the theatre and in the notions that had begun to prevail of what plays should be like. The public have always loved and will always love spectacle—the dumb-show and the background noises; there will also always be the critics with their opinions on the rights and wrongs of the production, and, as the French influence was now so powerful, notions about the impropriety of mixing the comic and the tragic, and about the general conduct of the plot, were confidently formulated as if critically inspired. Vulgar taste and learned opinion combined to encourage the actors to improve Shakespeare. To keep the stage going somehow in bad times is better than to shut down in despair of all amendment. There could therefore be no criticism had the mutilators of Shakespeare not been so pleased with themselves; they were not cynical in their improving; the distortions came from their souls.

Of the plays that were mutilated to fit them to Restoration taste *Macbeth* and *The Tempest* were amongst the first. Both provided opportunity for elaborate spectacle and music: the witch scenes in *Macbeth* and the magic of *The Tempest* allowed of almost operatic treatment. But not content with this form of decoration Davenant made additions to secure what he fancied was a more symmetrical plot. To balance Miranda he designed a man who had never seen a woman, and persuaded Dryden to help him with the botching. You may say that Shakespeare himself had pointed the way for some of these trespasses. *The Tempest* is in the form we have it something of a spectacle—but there is a place for spectacle on the stage when it is in keeping. *Macbeth*, however, as recent criticism has argued, may have been remodelled on more spectacular lines than those on which it was first designed. There is no need to argue the matter. Shakespeare may indeed at times have been forced to submit to what seemed certain necessities of the day; he must have known when he was writing *Hamlet* and some other of his longer pieces that they would not always be presented in their entirety on the stage; that there would have to be cuts must have occurred to him. He had his say, however, like Bach, and the pity is that as well as handing his papers to Heminge and Condell he did not put away copies in a drawer that could have been opened only in later times. If there ever was such a drawer, the jealous gods have seen to it that the key has been mislaid.

The most successful, if success can be measured by survival, of Restoration adaptations was Tate's *King Lear*. The wish to provide a happy ending to tragedies in which we feel strongly for the good is not unnatural. It is not surprising, therefore, that, like *Lear*, *Romeo and Juliet* was rewritten to accord

with this desire for poetical justice; yet that everyone might have it as they liked it *Romeo and Juliet*
was presented with a tragic and with a happy ending
night about. By Garrick's day *Romeo and Juliet* had
shed its alternative denouement, although the tragic
conclusion was now managed very differently from
that provided by Shakespeare. The happy ending to
*Lear*, however, still survived. Even Dr. Johnson
condoned the offence: 'Cordelia, from the time of
Tate, has always retired with victory and felicity',
he says, and adds the weight of his own feelings on
first reading *Lear* to the general suffrage that pre-
ferred Tate's adaptation to the original.

The last of the adaptations I should like to mention is Garrick's own version of *Hamlet* produced in
1772. This illustrates in a decisive manner the influence of French dramatic opinion, generally operative
throughout the period, on a particular actor and
producer.

Garrick had an ardent French admirer in Jean
François Ducis who kept continually before him a
portrait of his hero as Hamlet; and so powerfully did
this image operate on the fancy of Ducis that he
decided to make an acting version of *Hamlet* in
French. Ducis unfortunately knew no English whatever, but he did not allow this handicap to restrain
his progress: he had recourse to a French paraphrase

of *Hamlet* published by La Place in 1745 and trusted to his own enthusiasm and invention for the rest. Here in outline is the result:

Gertrude poisons her husband for the love of Claudius, and her son Hamlet becomes king. Hamlet cannot marry Ophelia, daughter of Claudius, for the Ghost has visited him off stage to tell him of the murder. Claudius conspires with Polonius to seize the throne. Gertrude, challenged by Hamlet to swear to her innocence on the urn containing her husband's ashes, faints and later does away with herself. Hamlet stabs Claudius to death as the latter leads an attack on the palace.

The most satisfactory feature about this effort by Ducis was that it made quite a small fortune for the penniless author; for Ducis is surely entitled to be called the author and given the credit, as he took the cash, for this remarkable invention. Talma made a reputation as the protagonist; those who wonder why the actor, depicted as Hamlet, is shown holding an urn must remember that this piece of classical furniture occupied a prominent place in the scene as redecorated by Ducis.

Garrick, who had so inspired his disciple and in other ways affected the French stage, was in his turn moved by French theatrical criticism and practice to refashion *Hamlet*; he hoped, by removing such vulgarities as the grave-diggers, and by generally raising the tone of the tragedy, to free Shakespeare from the aspersions of the critical and to placate French taste, which found such common ongoings in tragedy as the scene in the graveyard most unpalatable.

It was this and similar travesties of the plays that made Augustine Birrell exclaim:

It was not from the stage the voice arose bidding us recognise the supremacy of Shakespeare. Actors first ignored him then hideously mutilated him. Our gratitude is due in this great matter to men of letters.

Yet the actors were not the only guilty parties. Men of letters shared in the scandal. Dryden had helped Davenant to deface *The Tempest* and, in rewriting *Troilus and Cressida*, had not hesitated to declare that he was refining Shakespeare's language and eliminating the coarse and vulgar elements in the work. This was the cry of the next age, and Pope tried to give it practical expression in his edition of Shakespeare by degrading to the bottom of his pages what he judged to be vulgar and unworthy lines; in what he did retain of Shakespeare's text Pope frequently replaced Shakespeare's words by more genteel or elegant expressions. It will not do then to condemn the actors out of hand as the sole offenders. Dryden and Pope both admired Shakespeare; so did Garrick, and in his revision of *Hamlet* for the stage he was acting as his times prompted him. He listened to the critics and commentators—a very dangerous thing for an actor to do when it distracts his mind from the text, and fatal if he loses his trust in Shakespeare.

If I pause for a minute or two over Garrick, it is because his *Hamlet* is not without its lessons for us today. We must first, however, clear our minds of the idea that Garrick was, for all his faults, a mere figure of the stage. To help towards this I may remind you of a tribute to his powers from a contemporary whose testimony is authoritative.

Burke, for he is my authority, is, in the following passage from his letter to The Earl Fitzwilliam, anatomizing the folly of those who hope to come to terms with the newly formed Directory in France; for what are the five Directors and their two legislative bodies, he asks, but the same Ruffians, Thieves, Assassins, and Regicides that they were from the start of the Revolution; all they have done, Burke insists, is to change their costume, and he now glances at an amusing episode that accompanied this change of costume and draws his moral from some observations by Garrick on theatre decorum:

I remember in a conversation I once had with my ever dear friend Garrick, who was the first of Actors, because he was the most acute observer of nature I ever knew, I asked him how it happened that whenever a Senate appeared on the Stage, the Audience seemed always disposed to laughter. He said the reason was plain: the

Audience was well acquainted with the faces of most of the Senators. They knew that they were no other than candle-snuffers, revolutionary scene-shifters, second and third mob, prompters, clerks, executioners, who stand with their axe on their shoulders by the wheel, grinners in the Pantomime, murderers in Tragedies, who make ugly faces under black wigs; in short, the very scum and refuse of the Theatre; and it was of course that the contrast of the vileness of the Actors with the pomp of their Habits naturally excited ideas of contempt and ridicule.

The truth of Garrick's observation was confirmed for Burke by the conduct of the revolutionaries:

So it was at Paris on the inaugural day of the Constitution for the present year. The Diplomacy, who were a sort of strangers, were quite awestruck with 'the pride, pomp and circumstance' of this majestic Senate; whilst the Sansculotte Gallery instantly recognized their old insurrectionary acquaintance, burst out in a horse laugh at their absurd finery, and held them in infinitely greater contempt than whilst they prowled about the streets in the pantaloons of the last year's Constitution, when their Legislators appeared honestly, with their daggers in their belts and their pistols peeping out of the side pocket holes, like a bold brave Banditti, as they are.

It is a sketch of Garrick I contemplate with pleasure, even if he is only in the middle distance as it were beside his theatre, and one sees him across a foreground of social and political confusion.

There was no lack then in Garrick of native

observation and understanding; he was in addition a fair scholar, although Dr. Johnson, whose pupil he was, declared that he made out his Latin from the sense not the sense from the Latin; yet the critical ideas that were current made Garrick distrust Shakespeare, and the actor felt he was doing the dramatist a service by cutting out such vulgar characters as the grave-diggers from what was intended for a tragedy. It was not that the eighteenth century could not enjoy the vulgar, but it liked it all of a piece. Steevens, the Shakespeare scholar, writing to congratulate Garrick on his *Hamlet*, advised him not to dispose unthriftily of the orts and fragments he had left over from his carving of the play but to serve them up as a farcical after-piece; Steevens even suggested a title for this proposed concoction: *The Grave-diggers; with the pleasant Humours of Osrick, the Danish Macaroni.* The feeling that the dignity of tragedy demanded a more genteel vocabulary and handling than Shakespeare had always at his disposal was widespread. It even got as far as Scotland, and when Scotsmen ape what passes with the English as genteel we reach the genteel indeed.

David Hume was as good a Scotsman as ever wrote English, but he regarded Shakespeare as born in a barbarous age, and in his own *History* he thought it proper to transpose into the idiom of his own

enlightened day sayings that tradition had handed
down as the *ipsissima verba* of the men of those earlier
and less well-instructed times. One example is sufficient to illustrate his procedure. When Bruce was
hurrying to Scotland, to take up the work of libera-
tion begun by Wallace, he found an enemy in that
treacherous friend the Red Comyn. They met and
quarrelled in the church of the Blackfriars at Dum-
fries. Blows were exchanged, and Bruce came out to
say to his friends: 'I doubt I have slain the Red
Comyn.' 'Doubt!' said his companion Sir Thomas
Kirkpatrick, 'Doubt—I mak siccar' and in he went to
finish off, if necessary, the traitor. Hume, however,
shrank from repeating to the polite and cultivated
society of England and Edinburgh for which he
wrote so vulgar an expression as 'I mak siccar'; he
accordingly turned it as follows:

On one of his friends asking him if the traitor was slain
Bruce replied: 'I believe so'. 'And is that a matter', cried
Kirkpatrick, 'to be left to conjecture? I will secure him.'

I leave you to imagine what Kirkpatrick would have
said, could he have read Hume's account of the conversation. Yet Hume was no more a stupid or insensitive man than Garrick.

We have changed all that in England you may
say; and even France is beginning to admit Shakespeare's right to his own vocabulary. A glimpse, in

France's later and more romantic days, in 1886 to be precise, of a scene in the green-room of that fortress of tradition the *Comédie-Française* may serve as an epilogue to one phase of the reaction to Shakespeare. Paul Meurice, the friend and executor of Victor Hugo, is reading to the Selection Committee his own revision of Dumas's version of *Hamlet*. Dumas had from about December 1847 made a success at the *Théâtre Historique* with his adaptation. Meurice was now offering a much revised version to the Committee, a translation more faithful to the original. When Meurice came to his rendering of the passage, 'I do not set my life at a pin's fee', Augustine Brohan could stand such common words as 'pin' no longer and in a burst of laughter said: 'Ma vie, une épingle vaut mieux.' To this sally the translator replied: 'Madame, ce n'est pas de moi, c'est de Shakespeare.' When a French man of letters can silence a distinguished *sociétaire*, as she protests against the presence of vulgar expressions in a tragedy, with *c'est de Shakespeare*, we may conclude that we are reaching the end of an epoch.[1]

---

[1] In this account of the production of 1886 I am indebted to M. Paul Benchettrit, who has examined its stages in the still unpublished diary of the Director of the *Comédie-Française* at that time. For M. Benchettrit's generous permission to borrow here from his own unpublished work, and for suggestions elsewhere, I am most grateful.

In England, as in France, we have at last reversed a process that began immediately on Shakespeare's death. Even his colleagues Heminge and Condell, or their scribes, felt that in presenting the plays to the reader some modifications were not improper. The tougher stage versions were toned down accordingly. Later, this extended from the language to the play as a whole. There were not wanting voices to protest against this later vandalism; but we must remember that as some of the worst damage to our ancient buildings was done by restorers zealous for some ideal of architectural purity—as well as by merely vulgar vandals—so the mutilation of Shakespeare was in part at least prompted by scholarly pretensions. Scholarship has now put certain elements in the critical understanding of Shakespeare into a truer historical perspective, so that their relative importance can be better estimated. The modern actor and producer have a much sounder body of doctrine to guide them than was available to Garrick. If they err in certain matters, they do so because of their own ignorance or caprice; yet there are still many problems and still great dangers in translating the findings of scholars and men of letters too literally into the language of the stage.

How far the return to Shakespeare, to the whole Shakespeare, and to nothing but Shakespeare has gone today may be studied conveniently and usefully in Sir Laurence Olivier's film version of *Hamlet*. The convenience lies in our having in the film, since most of us have seen it for ourselves, a common reference point; the utility in this that the production was designed for performance before a larger and more mixed audience than any hitherto envisaged by a producer. By considering the film we might expect to discover what the producer reckoned was the highest common factor, if we can talk of such a thing in the artistic sphere, that he could count on in the various groups that would contribute to its success or failure in the cinema. As the film also happens to illustrate some of the difficulties that will always confront a producer of this play, and no less the relation between the scholarship of a period and its stage production, I propose to comment at some length on the film and refer only briefly to parallel stage productions.

I am not, I may remind you, interested at present in the question whether it was a good or a successful film. It was judged by those who should know to be both good and successful; and I must say I think that its banning by the Bulgarian Government after a brief but popular run is a testimony to something vital in its appeal that those who would impose an ideology on humanity find disturbing. I am to consider the film only in so far as it professes to offer us an interpretation of Shakespeare, and I try to discount all those features that arise from the play's translation into a medium so different from that for which it was written. I omit all consideration of the propriety of filming Shakespeare; it is enough for me that Shakespeare has been filmed and will be filmed, and that the film we are now to consider may suggest some questions of interpretation that are perhaps worth pondering.

Looking at the film as a help to estimating a common factor in the attitude to Shakespeare today over a wide range of audiences, you will admit, if you remember what has happened in the past, that the result is not discouraging. It is true that *Hamlet* has the power to appeal to all levels of understanding—from that of those who find their thrill in the Ghost or the fencing match to that of those who can see it all of a piece. Perhaps Mr. Alan Dent, in replying to some criticisms of his arrangement of the text, was not justified in arguing that to please 20 million cinema-goers he had to offend some 2,000 Shakespearian experts, unless he felt that in the two thousand there would be no judicious opinion that should outweigh whole cinemas of others; for he might have trusted more than he did to Shakespeare's power especially in *Hamlet* to please all even on the screen of today as on the boards of yesterday.

The film for all its merits yet shows in places the operation of forces that in earlier times made for distortion: the two apparently opposite tensions, the popular and the scholarly, can still be seen each pulling its own way. Let me begin then with a scene in which the producer deliberately as it were turns his back on Shakespeare to solicit popular applause; from there I shall pass to some difficult but crucial places in the management of the action where scholarly and popular opinion may be at cross purposes, and finally come to examine the influence that scholarship has shed over the basic conception of the production.

For the treatment of the nunnery scene in the film I can find no reasonable excuse, since I cannot see that there was anything here, either of time, or of circumstance, to prevent the film's following Shakespeare.

The exchanges between Hamlet and Ophelia that constitute the nunnery scene are prefaced by Hamlet's words, half spoken to himself, on his seeing Ophelia:

Nymph, in thy orisons be all my sins remembered.

The words suggest a very different attitude to her

from that displayed a few moments earlier by her father and the King as they dispose of her like a bait in a trap; and it is the immediate and emphatic contrast to their purely selfish use of the girl provided by Hamlet's words that satisfies me that we must reject any suggestion that Hamlet has overheard in an earlier scene the little plot proposed by Polonius. Hamlet's words are somewhat out of the ordinary, as critics have noted, but this is surely because Hamlet sees her for the moment as something apart from the rottenness infecting the Denmark of his musings. Ophelia provides the epilogue to the scene —like Hamlet's prologue a confession drawn from the speaker in the surprise of the moment—

O, what a noble mind is here o'erthrown!

Between these two as it were *sotto voce* passages— the inmost ponderings of their respective souls—lie the harsh exchanges, showing to begin with a certain constraint, and passing, as Hamlet gradually discovers the parts the King and Polonius are playing in the scene, into the unrestrained invective and threats for which Hamlet no longer hesitates to make Ophelia the vehicle. If you examine Shakespeare's text at this point, you will, I think, agree that in Shakespeare's presentation of the scene Ophelia is silenced but not overwhelmed by the torrent of the

Prince's denunciation; for like most women, when men let themselves rage against conduct that does not square with their masculine ideas, Ophelia thinks Hamlet is mad.

> O, heavenly powers, restore him!
> O help him, you sweet heavens!

are her well meant but to the recipient of these kindnesses, I fear, maddening reactions. When at last the Prince gives it up and storms out Ophelia expresses her feeling in lines in keeping with her earlier impression, for she now dwells on the pity of Hamlet's condition. True, she is sorry not only for Hamlet but for herself, as she had very proper hopes of being his wife. To see so promising a *parti* going to the bad would doubtless distress any nice girl; Ophelia's reactions are in the situation as natural as they are humane and becoming.

In the film the episode is managed very differently. As Hamlet departs, Ophelia, instead of speaking Shakespeare's words about

> The glass of fashion and the mould of form,
> The observed of all observers,

instead of translating the fury and invective of the Prince into the music of her own loving comment, without a word, casts herself down on the pavement writhing and howling horribly.

All else apart, this seems to show a sad misunderstanding of the character of Ophelia. Had relief from the pressure of grief and love come so easily to her and found its vent in such simple physical form her reason would not have suffered as it did. By itself, however, the film's treatment of the episode seems unjustifiable, although the device of casting oneself on the floor seems to have been in fashion about the time the film was in the making. This bit of business figured in a stage version of about the same date, but in the scene where Ophelia is distracted. Here too the action seemed uncalled for, though it was not substituted for an important part of the text. Yet in whatever manner Ophelia is played in that scene, the actress should have in mind the words of Laertes:

> Thought and affliction, passion, hell itself,
> She turns to favour and to prettiness.

Such tumblings may be very well in Shaw's *Apple Cart*, where persons and policies are prone to such upsets, but favour and prettiness are not the words we should apply to them.

One of the temptations in acting, as in editing or commenting on *Hamlet*, is to invent some new feature and, instead of allowing the old words and situations to recreate themselves anew in the imagination, to thrust this alien device or emendation or conclusion, according to one's business, on the spectator or reader, in the hope that he will feel he is enjoying a new and individual interpretation. In the stage version of *Hamlet* I speak of, what might have been a well-considered if not new idea was sadly marred by overplaying. King Claudius is, as we can all gather, too fond of the bottle. In the original Hamlet-story, from which Shakespeare borrowed, what is called strong drink has a natural place; the tale is a tough one and as in the modern hard-boiled story men drink. Mr. Somerset Maugham's comments on the hero of the latter-day type may recall for you its alchoholic atmosphere:

He has remarkable power of absorbing hard liquor. In the drawer of his desk there is always a bottle of rye or bourbon which he gets out whenever he has a caller and whenever he has nothing else to do. He keeps a flask in his hip-pocket and a pint in the glove-compartment of his car. The first thing when he arrives at an hotel is to send the bell-boy for a bottle.

Shakespeare's *Hamlet* has many of the ingredients of the hard-boiled story—the dramatist has not omitted the drink; but now it is the villain who is always calling for the equivalent of the modern daiquiris or stingers; indeed the King's intemperate habits provide Hamlet with the subject of a discourse that we must later consider in some detail. In the stage version I refer to the actor playing Claudius did make one realize the tougher side of the drama, and would have scored a valuable point had he remembered that the most ardent drinker has moments of an agonizing sobriety and distressing lucidity of mind. Such a moment we have surely in the scene that follows the revelation of the play-scene. Claudius now knows that Hamlet has somehow learnt of the murder and may well mean business. The King feels he must pray and tries to look at his deed as we may suppose heaven itself regards it. He may, only some minutes earlier, have been warm with drink; the feeling now is rather that of the morning after. Yet the actor, having till this point played the part well, came in to pray, a stoup in one hand and a pint-pot in the other, and after a couple of very quick ones fell on his knees, not, one felt, because he wished to pray but to prevent his legs from giving under him. Yet if ever the King is sober it is now, and it is this sobriety that gives emphasis to his predicament.

Putting aside the caprices of producer or actor we may pass to some of the difficulties that confront any modern producer of *Hamlet*. There is in the first scene as in the very opening of *Macbeth* a supernatural element to be dealt with. Perhaps the witches overtax the resources of the modern stage and the imagination of a modern audience. If witches are to be embodied for the modern play-goer they will hardly be

> So wither'd and so wild in their attire

as Shakespeare's, and the weird sister of today may be more *chez soi* at a cocktail party than on a blasted heath. But a ghost, in spite of protestations, is still a living presence in the popular imagination, though the dramatist may have to introduce it with care and tact. The screen, one might fancy, would provide the ideal mechanism for such an introduction; the camera makes possible a range of mere illusion beyond what can be compassed on the stage. The camera would doubtless serve admirably in *Hamlet*, if the Ghost could be shown in the habit fashionable today for a wraith, or even if it would act the fleeting phantom hurrying down a corridor. But Shakespeare's Ghost is too substantial for such impressionistic treatment; he is almost the principal person in the First Act, or at least so dominating that critics have asked themselves why Shakespeare insists on bringing this figure so prominently before us. A producer is not concerned to answer this question in critical terms; but, if he need not offer a solution in reasoned form, he has to feel the right answer in his own bones, if he is to make so unshrinking a phantom as Shakespeare's an acceptable and efficient participant in the drama.

The right approach to this question that producer as well as critic must face is perhaps suggested by a remark by Ibsen. Speaking of the play we call *Ghosts*, he said the French had found a title more suggestive of the idea of his drama: they called it *Les Revenants*. Shakespeare's Ghost is also a *revenant*, just as his witches are also the weird sisters. The Ghost comes to us therefore

> with that fair and warlike form
> In which the majesty of buried Denmark
> Did sometimes march.

As we examine Shakespeare's text we can see the care Shakespeare has taken in picturing for us the appearance of the Ghost; he was not content that the spectators should see it with their own eyes; they see it also through the eyes of the other characters. There was to be a kind of confirmation in the coincidence of the two pictures—the spectator could superimpose that given by the characters on his own. The timing of the Ghost's entries Shakespeare has calculated with equal care. Horatio and Marcellus are seated listening to Bernardo's story and, as they look towards the star to which he points and hear with the inward ear the bell beating one, the Ghost is on them, and they spring to their feet. This episode I have seen taken in such a way that the soldiers remain seated as they contemplate the Ghost. This can hardly be proper, for they are first of all a guard and now in the presence of the majesty of buried Denmark. Everything seems to require them to rise in haste; so doubt dispels itself in action, although the chill of reality may then as it were freeze them where they stand.

A study of the detail of the Ghost-scenes seems to confirm the paradox propounded by Granville-Barker: there is no illusion so there is every illusion. The Ghost had to walk on to the stage of *The Globe* soon after two o'clock in the full light of the early afternoon; all this Shakespeare has allowed for and transformed to dramatic gain. Yet on the screen where visual illusion can be so craftily employed the producer's problem so far from being easier may very well be insoluble. In the film the producer doubtless felt that amidst his realistic properties he must have a realistic ghost. The difficulty is to find someone who knows what a ghost is really like. On the stage itself a would-be realistic producer creates for himself the difficulty that seems inherent in the film. There is nothing to be gained by the Ghost's speaking in an asthmatic kind of way or between consumptive chokings. The King is dead; he is not about to die or in need of medical attention. His physical infirmities have been cast off, and it is in virtue of something vital and commanding that he returns

again. Realistic ghosts that cannot possibly har-
monize with the text far from creating destroy all
illusion; and what is worse cannot sustain the part
in the drama designed for them by Shakespeare.

The Ghost, like every other character in the play,
may be looked at from one or other of two points of
view; it is from one side a piece of mechanism fitted
into a complete machine, to be judged by the effi-
ciency with which it takes up or transmits the power
that is generated by the plant as a whole; from the
other it is an end in itself. It is just like a buttress in
a building, which is a mere prop or pin sustaining a
stress or anchoring a mass to solid earth and yet, in
the great creations of the Ile-de-France, a miraculous
flight of stone lifting its load to the heavens, as at
Reims, with angels' wings. As a piece of mechanism
in the plot the Ghost is indispensable. Shakespeare
requires a murder that shall be secret and yet known to
Hamlet, one that only the murderer or the murdered
could reveal to him. The Ghost is the mechanism of
communication. This aspect of the plot has naturally
attracted the attention of those interested in the
detective story; the circumstances, the drug, the
discovery of the crime, have been examined by such
experts as Mr. Simpson or Mr. Stewart. All that I
have to say now on this aspect of the matter is that
Shakespeare employs his Ghost economically: the

Ghost is not there merely for the thrill of it. The machine could not function without him. The Ghost, however, is much more than a cog in the mechanism of the plot. He is a moral agent in the drama, an individual in his own artistic right. Just as the buttresses at Chartres or Reims have assumed the forms they have not merely from mechanical necessity but at the dictate of art, so the Ghost's participation in the play is governed by an idea of which the plot itself is only a function.

Can we then say something intelligible and brief about this idea that I venture to say dictates the treatment of the Ghost? I think it is possible if you will allow me to employ as a kind of shorthand another man's terminology. The form of a literary work, says Professor Trilling, is an idea, and we have an idea, he continues, when two contradictory emotions are made to confront each other and are required to have a relationship with each other. Can we then in *Hamlet* pick out two contradictory emotions that are required to have a relationship with one another, or find, in place of these emotions, an opposition of ideals that must conform to the same law?

Turning to the play to look for the opposites from whose dialectic the work is generated we find what seems at first sight a strange diversity of elements.

The basic story comes down to us from early Germanic times and is touched with the chill and starkness of Icelandic saga; yet such additions to the basic material as the actors walk into this tale of a bygone age as naturally as if they were visiting Elsinore in the days of Queen Elizabeth. There is what Henry James would call a very remarkable instance of foreshortening in this picture that may repay examination. Henry James's own definition of foreshortening, as

representation arrived at not by the addition of items but by the art of figuring synthetically, a compactness into which the imagination may cut thick, as into the rich density of a wedding cake,

may leave us somewhat mystified; yet his imagery, though perhaps very Victorian, as even wedding cake is probably not quite what it used to be, hints at his meaning, and a consideration of the picture itself should help us to develop his suggestions.

How careful Shakespeare has been to avoid all distortion with the perspective of his foreshortening is clearly seen when even a master hand tries to redraw some of the parts. Goethe in the character of his Wilhelm Meister discusses the lines on which he thinks the play might with advantage be redesigned. He begins by distinguishing between the essential features of the play, 'the grand internal relations of the persons and events' and what he calls the external relations, the accidents that take one character to Poland and another to France or England. Amongst these external relations, as Goethe sees them, is Horatio's coming from Wittenberg or Hamlet's design to return there. Wilhelm is impelled to unify as it were, or rationalize in some way, these various but secondary or external relations. This scattering young men over Europe seems too arbitrary when the plot might be redesigned to keep them on one well marked route, and Goethe secures this uniformity by a revision that he summarized as follows:

After the death of Hamlet's father, the Norwegians, lately conquered, grow unruly. The viceroy of that country sends his son Horatio, an old school-friend of Hamlet's, and distinguished above every other for his bravery and prudence, to Denmark, to press forward the equipment of the fleet, which, under the new luxurious King, proceeds but slowly. Horatio has known the former King, having fought in his battles, having ever stood in favour with him—a circumstance by which the first ghost-scene will be nothing injured. The new sovereign gives Horatio audience and sends Laertes into Norway with intelligence that the fleet will soon arrive; whilst Horatio is commissioned to accelerate the preparation of it; and the Queen, on the other hand, will not consent that Hamlet, as he wishes, should go to sea along with him.

'Heaven be praised!' cried Serlo; 'we shall now get rid

of Wittenberg and the university, which was always a sorry piece of business.'

For our present purpose we need go no farther with Goethe's suggestions, only note that in the same discussion Goethe has shown how in what seem small and unimportant details we may discover Shakespeare's greatness as a dramatist; and this he illustrates by showing how the proposal to save personnel by reducing Rosencrantz and Guilden-stern to one person reveals a lack of understanding of Shakespeare's art. Rosencrantz or Guildenstern appearing alone might give the impression that here was an individual with unique characteristics, whereas Shakespeare wishes us to see that their sycophancy and outlook are common and abundant; to effect this there must be more than one of the kind on view, and they must be almost indistinguishable from one another. In attributing to Shakespeare so nice a sense of detail Goethe might have reflected that the introduction of Wittenberg and its univer-sity was not without its significance and that, in his zeal for keeping the young men travelling on a uniform path between Denmark and Norway, he was obliterating another of those small touches that reveal the master's grasp of detail and his power of ordering everything in the interests of the total effect.

It is unnecessary to enlarge on how characteristic of Laertes it is that he should go to Paris, or of Fortinbras that he fight in Poland, or of Horatio that he come from Wittenberg; but with Goethe's criticism in mind something further should perhaps be said of the contribution of Wittenberg to the idea of the play.

The importance of the university becomes clear only towards the end of the first act. The opening scene explains to us why Denmark is engaged on a rearmament drive, and why the soldiers think the visitations of the Ghost may have some connexion with the danger threatening the country. Hamlet's father had accepted the challenge of Fortinbras of Norway to mortal combat; each had staked an ample territory on his prowess; and Norway now threatened to dispute Denmark's possession of what Hamlet had gained for it by slaying Fortinbras. This explanation provides us with some knowledge of the character and interests of Hamlet's father and of the times he lived in. Neither of the combatants in the duel that started the trouble was, it is clear, a university man, nor would it seem that either had academic interests. Certainly the Ghost brings no scholarly airs to the platform he revisits. If the first scene is the Ghost's, the second is Hamlet's, and it is here we learn of Wittenberg and its attractions for Hamlet.

This taken with what we see of him for ourselves satisfies us that he is a scholar, so that when father and son meet in the closing scenes of the act, not merely two types, but two ages confront one another. Wittenberg—the University—is face to face with the heroic past. From this opposition are generated the two conflicting emotions that constitute the idea that informs the play.

Shakespeare's arrangement of the ideals of these two ages in depth within his scenic frame, instead of placing them apart at the opposite extremities of his canvas, is what Henry James means by foreshortening or figuring synthetically. It is not, as some have argued, confusing or confounding different periods. In all periods different ages meet; the notion that Shakespeare has secured an unreal opposition by introducing the civilized present into a dead past is possible only to those so remote from realities that they fancy civilization maintains its footing in the world thanks to the goodwill of the uncivilized.

Should you accept even in part the argument as so far presented, you must agree that it will not do to show us Hamlet talking to a kind of skeleton from the grave or a wheezing, coughing creature that will soon be there. However the scene is managed, careful attention must be given to the words Shakespeare has written for the situation. Nothing but disappointment can come from our turning our backs on the text and trusting to our own ingenuity; the alterations or amendments to the action suggested even by men of genius now seem almost comic in their ineptitude; we should be warned by such examples and remember we alter Shakespeare at our peril.

It may, you could reply, be difficult to present the Ghost to a modern audience, but little need be lost, you might add, for everyone can see for themselves the opposition set up in Hamlet's mind by the Ghost's injunction. Wittenberg, you might continue, is the label that informs us of the particular brand of melancholy Shakespeare is going to entertain us with. The university has implanted or fostered that inability to act to which at the very start the film directs our attention. We are to see, we are told, the tragedy of a man who could not make up his mind. Any truth, therefore, in the contrast so far drawn between Hamlet and his father is implicit in the production; one need not, therefore, worry too much about the make-up of the Ghost.

To this I must reply that you have mistaken the nature of the opposition I have in mind; the contrast is not between a very tough father and a foot-in-the-grave young man; Wittenberg does not stand for donnish indecision, for I do not think Shakespeare

regarded the university as a symbol of the ineffectual
—Horatio you must remember was also a university
man. When, however, I go on to suggest that the
contrast is nothing so simple as that between
thought and action, you may draw my attention to
Hamlet's own words that the producer has used as
a Prologue to the play:

> So, oft it chances in particular men
> That, for some vicious mole of nature in them,
> As in their birth, wherein they are not guilty,
> Since nature cannot choose his origin;
> By the o'ergrowth of some complexion,
> Oft breaking down the pales and forts of reason;
> Or by some habit that too much o'er-leavens
> The form of plausive manners—that these men,
> Carrying, I say, the stamp of one defect,
> Being nature's livery or fortune's star,
> His virtues else, be they as pure as grace,
> As infinite as man may undergo,
> Shall in the general censure take corruption
> From that particular fault.

Hamlet provoked by the King's debauchery is here
commenting on the bad name his countrymen get for
themselves by their intemperance, and that in spite
of all their virtues. This, you may add, is only the
ostensible subject of his discourse: Hamlet, though
he is referring to the mote in the eye of his com-
patriots, is all unbeknown to himself directing us

to the beam in his own eye. He is really providing us with an analogue to the fault that causes the tragedy —his own inability to make up his mind because of the over-reflective habit fostered at Wittenberg.

Were I now to say that I do not doubt the truth of Hamlet's generalization, only the producer's judgement in applying the words to Hamlet himself and in using the passage as a Prologue to the play, the producer might very well reply that he was a busy man and that I could argue the matter with the many distinguished scholars whose interpretations of the speech had suggested to him its use as a Prologue; and, he might add, that it was unlikely that an interpretation of tragedy that goes back to Aristotle (for surely 'the particular fault' is just the *hamartia* of Aristotle) can be challenged, with any reason, at this late day.

Hamlet's words, as adapted by the producer for his Prologue to the film, do offer a succinct and no doubt persuasive formulation of what may be called the orthodox interpretation of Tragedy; and the producer, though no doubt agreeing that this interpretation has not escaped criticism, might claim that for every scholarly critic that could be called against it he could cite a dozen on its behalf. Were it to be objected that judgement here cannot be arrived at by counting heads, there is the obvious retort that

there is no lack of authority amongst those that support the producer's judgement, for do they not include such names as Aristotle and Bradley? I turn
then first of all to examine the most authoritative of
those who seem to support the producer's interpretation of Tragedy; after hearing their testimony we
shall consider the evidence that Shakespeare himself
provides on the question now at issue.

# II

## THE SUBSTANCE OF TRAGEDY

WHEN one has grown old and hardened in any particular calling it is difficult to forget one's purely professional interests. Listening to the opening words of the Prologue to the film,

> So, oft it chances in particular men . . .

I could not help looking forward to what the prophetic voice would make of the famous crux towards the end of the passage, where the 'dram of eale' that has so befuddled the commentators is introduced. Needless to say spirits from the vasty deep, or as here from the obscurity of cloudy heights, do not condescend to this mundane detail. The voice stops just where the textual problem begins, and leaves us no excuse for postponing consideration of the dramatic significance of the speech.

In the lines the producer offers us as the key to the play, Hamlet, provoked by the drunkenness of the King, is commenting on a fault in his countrymen that draws on them the censure of the world, and so soils their reputation that their virtues lose all colour and commendation. This is the ostensible subject of Hamlet's discourse, but the producer would contend that it touches a deeper and more hidden matter: Hamlet all unconsciously is drawing our attention to the tragic flaw in his own character, the fault that the situation he is to find himself in will discover for us, the cause of the catastrophe. And the producer might observe that he is in his reading of the passage taking full advantage of the best academic lights. Many excellent scholars have subscribed to this view, and it must be admitted that in taking Hamlet's lines in this way we have a very neat and persuasive application of the time-honoured doctrine of *hamartia*. Shakespeare, it might be argued, is merely expanding for us in his own vigorous style the passage in Aristotle's *Poetics* that insists on the *hamartia* or fault in the tragic hero. We need not suppose that Shakespeare had Aristotle in mind: it would perhaps be even more satisfying were we to be persuaded that Shakespeare is providing independent confirmation of an idea that had occurred to the critic; for where Aristotle and Shakespeare agree who would have the temerity or impertinence to differ? Besides, the tenor of the lines is so obviously in tune with Hamlet's nature as transcribed by the commentators, it so confirms, and is confirmed by, traditional criticism of the play and the character, that argument seems unnecessary.

The producer's claim so far is not to be denied; all I ask is that we look again at the play and the criticism for ourselves, not, however, in the spirit of those who must contradict whatever tradition has handed down or of those who believe wisdom was born only with their generation or indeed with themselves. Superior enlightenment of this sort is a mere will-o'-the-wisp that plays over the fatuity and ignorance of mankind. Yet, I may remind you, there have been great revolutions in the domains of art; principles that once seemed axiomatic have had to be reconsidered, and this could be illustrated very easily from the history of Shakespearian criticism itself. What was once so confidently affirmed may now in parts be as confidently denied. Our criticism of Shakespeare, if it is to have any vital significance, must grow from our own study, however firmly that is grafted on tradition. It is in this belief that I venture now to examine with you one of those great prepossessions which so many generations have brought to their reading or study of Shakespeare. It is a prepossession that we cannot very well dismiss as a subject fit only for the wrangling of pedants. What stands writ so large on the front of a film of *Hamlet* that some 20 million people have enjoyed may be said to have qualified for discussion in the Lord Northcliffe lectures.

Looking first at Hamlet's speech in its context in the play, we may note that it comes before Hamlet has received the Ghost's message and command. Hamlet is not aware of any particular duty that he has neglected; if he is indeed touching unconsciously on some defect in his own nature, he is anticipating what is to become plain only in the sequel; we must then regard his remarks as prophetic. Quite apart moreover from any reference to himself Hamlet's words are sufficiently relevant: it is natural for men in such a situation as that in which Hamlet and his companions find themselves to fasten on some topic apparently unconnected with the business that holds them in suspense. The sounds of revelry that come at least to the mind's ear from the halls below and the suggestions of light and warmth and conviviality that accompany them provide a perfect foil for the exposed and anxious group on the battlements. Shakespeare here achieves one of those studies in darkness and light with which painters and poets so often quicken our imagination. Nor is the topic of the discussion without its significance in the setting of the play as a whole; it has more than a scenic value. The suggestion has already been made that Shakespeare has not emphasized the drinking habits of the court without set purpose. He has no time to spare, however, for showing us the royal party at the festive board; we have to realize that feature of the background from the hints that obtrude on our notice in the conversation of the actors in the piece. The King when immediately before us is never in his cups; for I have not yet heard it suggested that he missed the dumb-show because he had just dined too well. Shakespeare, however, has to fasten in our minds the idea of a self-indulgent King, and in this moment of suspense for us as for the characters he secures this effect as he heightens our sense of the scene before us by providing a contrasting feature.

Should you still feel that Shakespeare may have extracted more from the situation, even to the extent of defining tragedy for us, you must admit, if you regard the lines as a formulation of the doctrine of *hamartia*, how wide and all-inclusive his definition is. One phrase is sufficient to make this clear. The fault can be either Nature's livery or Fortune's star. Here Hamlet is making one of the favourite distinctions of his age. In *As You Like It* Rosalind explains the difference between Nature and Fortune to Celia: 'Fortune reigns in the gifts of the world, not in the lineaments of Nature.' Nature dressed you in the features and limbs you were born with; the clothes you have on and the money in your pocket are Fortune's gift. The vicious mole Hamlet talks of may come from Nature—'As in their birth,' says Hamlet, and adds

> wherein they are not guilty,
> Since nature cannot choose her origin.

Cleopatra's shapely nose, which Pascal suggested had almost changed the face of the world, was Nature's gift—she could hardly be guilty on that score. Yet Hamlet's train of thought had been fired by a fault that can hardly be regarded as exempt from moral censure or at least disapprobation; drunkenness is elsewhere loathsome to Hamlet. Taking Hamlet's words in detail you can stretch the notion of *hamartia*, if that is their connotation, so far that it can include every kind of blemish from a squint to a propensity to murder.

Still you may say there is in Hamlet's words something that reminds us of Aristotle. Shakespeare has suggested a line of thought or created an undercurrent of reflection that flows in a direction already surveyed by Aristotle.

Turning to Aristotle himself we find that scholars, whose learning provides the spectacles that enable us to read the text, allow between them as much latitude to the meaning of *hamartia* as Hamlet seems to do to the 'dram of eale'. Some regard *hamartia* as just a bad shot; others regard it as a moral flaw. Later we must try to look at the matter for ourselves; meantime it is enough to remember how inclusive scholarly interpretation of Aristotle's words tends

to be, and that the scholars are as all-embracing as
Hamlet in his treatment of human faults and frailties.
Macbeth's assassination of his sovereign and guest
is certainly a fault; but Juliet's fibs to her father have
been regarded as not perhaps equally heinous yet
equally a fault; in the tragic nexus the result is the
same, for Juliet like Macbeth is dead before the story
ends, and we must judge, it seems, by results.

As we pause in our reluctance to equate what seem
disproportionate causes, we come upon a further
device designed to help us over this difficulty raised
by the nature of the tragic flaw. The whole point of
tragedy, we are told, lies in the want of proportion
between cause and effect: the cause and the catastrophe are not commensurable. It is impossible to
equate Juliet's fibs or Ophelia's confidences to her
father—for girls that tell their father all may come
to as unhappy an end as those that keep their fathers
sweet with soothing stories—with their fate. It is
true in life itself, and certainly in the city I come
from, that failing to look both ways before you cross
the street may have fatal consequences; yet you cannot build a tragedy as Aristotle defined it, and as the
masters of that kind design it, on such an error.
There would be wanting another element in the
work that Aristotle regarded not merely as an essential feature but as the very end or purpose of the

dramatist's art: this he called *catharsis*. For the moment let us assume that by this idea Aristotle meant something like reconciliation or redemption. Now it was and is in the interests of this reconciliation or redemption that Aristotle did and later commentators do introduce the notion of *hamartia*. For how if there is no fault, it is asked, shall we be reconciled to the protagonist's fate? We are not rebellious, we are told, at the spectacle the tragic artist presents to us, because we see a reason in it that satisfies our moral sense. Any kind of reason will not do, since we can find no satisfaction at all in the slaughter of the young and the old that our roads see daily, although we can see the reason for it only too clearly. There is no sense of satisfaction or reconciliation, or there should be none, in such a murderous chronicle. We cannot therefore be satisfied, when we complain of the lack of proportion between the fault and the catastrophe, with the reply that that is just how the world goes. We know well enough that the world does not seem to move on lines that satisfy our ethical notions, and we are far from reconciled to its facts. To offer us then any kind of fault will not serve; and if there is no need for any proportion between fault and fate we may well ask why there need be any flaw at all. The vehicle that runs you over might kill you on the pavement itself as you were in the very act of looking both ways. To introduce a flaw in the attempt to stop our asking difficult questions is unsatisfactory, since it merely provokes other and even more perplexing inquiries. Certainly Christian doctrine does not try to justify its faith by saying you will get what you deserve in this life. But faith does believe in a final balance. Take away the faith and we must, you may say, try to find another form of compensation; but I make bold to say you will not find it in any doctrine of *hamartia*.

Am I then, you may ask, one of those modern commentators who have thrown over their allegiance to Andrew Cecil Bradley? Do I find him as out of date as so many of the brighter spirits of our time do? Let me reassure you or confirm your worst suspicions that I am thoroughly old-fashioned. I still think Bradley's method genuinely critical and illuminating; I do not agree with those who feel he could not read Shakespeare properly because he had not taken a course from some book or other on how to read the poets. Nor do I see that Bradley suffered from the fault that has been so regularly put upon him recently, that of divorcing the characters from their context. Bradley like Maurice Morgann has been charged with the sort of childishness that makes listeners ring up the B.B.C. when someone's grandmother in a serial is described as having been knocked down by a motor-car. The B.B.C. receives telegrams, we are told, saying, 'Don't let granny die', and in America these messages would be accompanied, I am led to believe, by baskets of fruit and by cordials suitable for invalids. And if Bradley does seem at times to offend there is nothing new in the criticism of this form of fault. One irreverent critic distressed by the famous Note B in *Shakespearean Tragedy*—'Where was Hamlet at the time of his father's death?'—asked, 'Where was Hamlet when the light went out?' This line of criticism is as old as the book itself. Yet both Maurice Morgann and Bradley, while they examined the context with microscopic care, preserved a wonderful balance and breadth of judgement.

Modern critics of Bradley, although they have dwelt so frequently on what they consider his over-emphasis on character, have had little to say on the central doctrine of *Shakespearean Tragedy*. This doctrine, in spite of its enthusiastic reception and wide acceptance, for every modern critic who talks of the tragic flaw is, if he has considered the matter seriously, a student of Bradley—this doctrine, even in Bradley's own day, did not give universal satisfaction. Walter Raleigh, who followed Bradley first at Liverpool and then at Glasgow, never criticizes the doctrine as Bradley's, but when he says

The attempt to find a theoretic basis for the great tragedies has never been attended with the smallest success . . . the Shakespearean drama is an instrument of expression incomparably fuller and richer than the tongs and the bones of moralists and metaphysicians—

for 'moralists and metaphysicians' you may read, I fancy, Hegelians, and that includes Bradley. Raleigh's successor at Glasgow, Macneile Dixon, took an equally unfavourable view of moralists and metaphysicians in his *Tragedy*. Yet their criticism of Bradley has been little developed, although it touches what is central in his interpretation. We shall have occasion later on to see that Bradley has been criticized today because he did not base his findings on the moralists and metaphysicians of the Elizabethan age, but as this criticism is directed against Bradley because his notion of *hamartia* is judged not strict enough we shall come to it only after some consideration of his general position. The question we are now to address ourselves to is this: Has Bradley given the doctrine of *hamartia* some turn that relieves it of the objections so far urged against it? Bradley like Aristotle and Hegel insists that tragedy effects a reconciliation or produces a sense of redemption; how then does he overcome the difficulty about the lack of correspondence between the flaw and the catastrophe? It is a fault not to look both ways, but such omissions though they may explain do not reconcile us to the death of the pedestrian. Has Bradley isolated the factor in tragedy that allows us to look upon the conclusion with other eyes than those with which we so regularly contemplate the brutalities of existence?

Bradley begins by insisting that the hero always contributes in some measure to the disaster in which he perishes. A man or girl, let us say, becomes a soldier and is killed in the course of duty—have they contributed in some measure to their fate because they did not stay at home? But Bradley does not mean contribute in this sense. The tragic figure must show a fatal tendency to identify his whole being with one interest, object, passion, or habit of mind. Suppose then our soldier had a tendency in action to identify his whole being with winning the battle, a tendency that proved fatal. Has he contributed to his own destruction? Again the answer must be no, for there are these further qualifications:

The critical action is, in a greater or less degree, wrong or bad. The catastrophe is the return of the action on the head of the agent. It is an example of Justice.

Of poetical justice there is no account, and of human justice hardly any, for there is no pretence that the punishment fits the crime. We should be back where we started, were it not for a further assumption.

We are, Hegel and Bradley urge, to regard the Cosmos as an ethical substance—so ethical that it can tolerate nothing short of perfection. This substance finds the tragic hero identifying himself in a whole-hearted way with some particular object or passion. Antigone is determined to give her brother the rites of burial; Romeo and Juliet are devoted lovers. Such determinations and devotions the ethical substance judges too narrow and imperfect and wipes them out. No plea for mitigation of sentence on the score of merit or loyalty will serve: the more devoted the more culpable. At the end, however, we have, so we are told, a sense of reconciliation because what is denied is, so it is asserted, the exclusive and wrongful assertion of some right. The total right has engulfed the divided rights.

Bradley's elaboration of the Hegelian thesis has had a strong attraction for scholars and men of letters. Yet it shows no respect for the virtues of men; the best are doomed because not wholly perfect. This Cosmos that sentences the good and the true to death with as little compunction as it shows to the wicked resembles in one important respect the imaginings of the arch-pessimist among the great historians. Tacitus lays it down at the beginning of his *History*, as the thesis his account of affairs will sustain, that the gods care not for the happiness of mortals, only for their punishment: 'non esse curae deis securitatem nostram, esse ultionem.' Bradley's Cosmos resembles in its passion for retribution the gods of Tacitus: it cares only for the punishment of men. Bradley in his zeal to reconcile us to the facts of tragedy offers us a conclusion to which only a profound pessimism could possibly reconcile us.

That Bradley had no more intention than Hegel of maintaining a pessimistic doctrine is clear from his work as a whole; mingling with his main thesis are currents of thought from a different source; many of his most characteristic utterances flatly contradict the premises on which his argument rests. Lest you think I am trying to make out a case for the sake of argument, let me quote a passage from the indictment of Bradley by Professor Lily Campbell that I promised earlier to consider with you. She almost alone amongst the moderns ventures to criticize his central doctrine. Her charge is that Bradley is not a whole-hearted hamartian, if we may coin such an expression. Here are some of the counts in the accusation:

Bradley's analysis of the characters of tragedy was made on a foundation of morality without morals as well as a psychology untrue to psychological thinking of any period. For instance he speaks of this tendency to identify the whole being with one interest, object, passion, or habit of mind as a fatal gift which carries with it a touch of greatness.

The statement that Bradley worked on a foundation of morality without morals would have surprised not only Bradley but the Balliol from which he came, the Balliol that prided itself on its philosophy, the Balliol of Nettleship and Green of the *Prolegomena to Ethics*. As to Bradley's psychology being untrue to the psychological thinking of any period, it seems to have passed well enough in his own day and to remain more or less intelligible. As we shall see later Professor Campbell thinks his psychology should square with that of certain Tudor psychologists, if it is to explain Shakespeare's characterization. For the moment, however, I wish to dwell on what Professor Campbell regards as Bradley's chief offence: his notion that what he calls the tragic flaw may be at the same time the source of the hero's greatness. There seems to her a 'mystery' in this conclusion that conflicts with the simple dogmatic propositions into which she would like to resolve existence and its problems.

That Professor Campbell's arraignment of Bradley was provoked by an inconsistency in his doctrine I do not doubt. But this does not mean that Bradley's was a morality without morals, only that he found more things in Shakespeare than were allowed for in

Hegel's philosophy. Bradley, although he is the most thorough exponent of the doctrine of *hamartia*, indeed just because he makes so determined an effort to provide for it a philosophic and psychological basis, has to keep looking beyond it to interpret the tragedies. He is divided between Hegel and Shakespeare. Professor Campbell has detected the vacillation and charges him with deviationism. For Bradley feels he must ask the question, 'Why is it that a man's virtues help to destroy him?'; and for the moment at least he is no hamartian.

It would be tedious to illustrate in detail the contradictory aspects of Bradley's doctrine; I must, however, draw your attention to one feature in the arrangement of his argument that may help to explain to you how the contradictions arise. The chapter in *Shakespearean Tragedy* dealing with *The Substance of Tragedy* concludes with this note:

Partly in order not to anticipate later passages, I abstained from treating fully here the question why we feel, at the death of the tragic hero, not only pain but reconciliation and sometimes even exultation. As I cannot at present make good this defect, I would ask the reader to refer to the word *Reconciliation* in the Index.

Turning to the index you will find that the references are neither numerous nor extensive; but they provide the corrective to the scheme Bradley has tried to construct for us. At times they cancel out much of what he has already said, for we come on sentences of this tenor:

The impression [at the end of a tragedy is] that the heroic being, though in one sense and outwardly he has failed, is yet in another sense superior to the world in which he appears.

Further, anyone who asserts that Shakespeare's tragedies are un-Christian in their outlook should consider carefully Bradley's observation that the feeling of the hero's having risen superior to the demands of a merely mundane morality seems to imply an idea which if developed would transform the tragic view of things. In short the chapter on *The Substance of Tragedy* does not deal with its real substance or the essential being of the form; this is only dealt with later; the chapter that claims to deal with the substance merely describes certain accidental features whose significance depends on the substance to which they belong.

Bradley's speculations on *Reconciliation* naturally offend Professor Campbell, who is for having everything resolved into some disease of the mind or soul. To her

tragedies teach by *exempla* how to avoid ruin and misery by avoiding the loose and ungoverned passions which lead thereto. . . . Dramatic tragedies are, therefore, the most effective method of teaching by *exempla* the lessons of moral philosophy.

Words like *catharsis* and 'reconciliation' find no place in her index. Those great explorers of the human soul the tragic artists have shrunk to preachers whose business it is to recommend a safe standard of conduct by means of cautionary tales.

Bradley gave only a subordinate place in his exposition of tragedy to 'reconciliation' or what Aristotle calls *catharsis*. This word Aristotle himself uses once only in the *Poetics*, but it is the key to his defence of the drama against Plato's attack. The notion of *hamartia* or the tragic flaw is of secondary importance, being introduced to serve as an explanation of *catharsis*. The terms are not on a par with one another: *catharsis* is the name given to a variety of experience; *hamartia* is a form of hypothesis put forward to account for the phenomenon. Till we get this distinction clear we can hardly hope to escape the tangle in which Bradley finds himself. His difficulties come from his putting the cart before the horse. We must first examine the phenomenon, and then we may be in a position to judge the value of the explanation that is offered us. In *The Substance of Tragedy* Bradley deals only with *hamartia*; *catharsis* is added in a footnote. If we are to get the elements of the problem in their proper order we must begin with *catharsis*, and I shall now venture on this difficult topic, for, however inadequate the treatment, on some such ground all reasonable interpretations of tragedy must rest.

The first and major difficulty in this inquiry, you may point out to me, is the precise meaning we are to give to the word *catharsis*. On whose authority do I keep translating it as 'reconciliation' or 'redemption'? For are there not almost as many meanings to this word as there are scholars? 'A great historical discussion has centred round the phrase', says Butcher, and he adds, 'No passage, probably, in ancient literature has been so frequently handled by commentators.'

Like the search for the origins of tragedy the tracking of *catharsis* to its primal significance can take us back into a mysterious world where the golden bough still hung in the sacred grove. The word may have had reference to some ritual purification; and as Professor Gilbert Murray has insisted again and again the Dionysus ritual was a *catharsis*— a purification of the community from the taints and poisons of the old year. Such scholarly exploration is exciting and may be instructive, but it must be left to those properly equipped for the difficulties of the journey, especially if we can come by some understanding of Aristotle's use of the word by a more direct approach.

The scholarly examination of Aristotle's use of the word elsewhere than in the *Poetics* is, of course, important, but it cannot be said to have yielded any definite and generally accepted conclusions that are at the same time intelligible to a layman like myself. One must admire the learning and scholarship in the exhaustive study of the word by Hicks or Butcher, and yet one may not feel greatly enlightened on the one essential point—Aristotle's use of the word in the *Poetics*. Certain subsidiary features Butcher and others do make clear to us: that Aristotle was deliberately using the word in a metaphorical sense (which he promised in the *Politics* to explain in his treatise on Poetry); that its technical use in medicine was familiar, yet this was not the sense in which Aristotle employed it or he would not have had to promise to elaborate his meaning later. After a close and learned analysis Butcher concludes:

> Let us assume, then, that the tragic *Katharsis* involves not only the idea of emotional relief, but the further idea of the purifying of the emotions so relieved.

Butcher after all feels he can do no more than assume; and it must be confessed that his assumption is not easily understood. Earlier he had said:

Pity and fear are purged of the impure element which clings to them in life.

The results of the inquiry about the various meanings of *catharsis* are, it must be admitted, disappointing.

Turning to examine *hamartia* Butcher emphasizes its subordinate place to *catharsis* in Aristotle's argument:

With the exception of the definition of tragedy itself, probably no passage in the *Poetics* has given rise to so much criticism as the description of the tragic hero in ch. xiii. The qualities requisite to such a character are here deduced from the primary fact that the function of tragedy is to produce the *katharsis* of pity and fear; pity being felt for a person who, if not wholly innocent, meets with suffering beyond his deserts; fear being awakened when the sufferer is a man of like nature with ourselves.

Butcher arranges the elements of the problem in their significant order: we must start from the primary fact—*catharsis*. The scholar, however, soon finds himself confronted by the difficulty we have already encountered—the nature of the tragic flaw. 'A moral error', Butcher observes,

A moral error easily shades off into a mere defect of judgment. But that mere defect may work as potently as crime. Good intentions do not make actions right. The lofty disinterestedness of Brutus cannot atone for his want of practical insight.

And having arrived at the old problem of the lack of correspondence between cause and catastrophe the Greek scholar takes refuge in the Bradleian remark:

> In the scheme of the universe a wholly unconscious error violates the law of perfection; it disturbs the moral order of the world. Distinctions of motive—the moral guilt or purity of the agent—are not here in question. So too in tragedy those are doomed who innocently err no less than those who sin consciously.

We have here a moral order that recognizes no moral distinctions—the accusation Professor Campbell levels at Bradley—yet at the end the same ambiguity that we find in Bradley:

> The tragic irony sometimes lies precisely herein, that owing to some inherent frailty or flaw—it may be human short-sightedness, it may be some error of blood or judgment—the very virtues of a man hurry him forward to his ruin.

We have again reached the point from which we wished to return to make a fresh start: faults are once more turning into virtues. Butcher in his study of *catharsis* and *hamartia* gets their relation to each other right, but he still leaves us in the tangle of Bradley's doctrine.

In our difficulty over *catharsis* there seems open to us only one promising resource, and this may be illustrated from that part of Aristotle's writings that deal with his biological interests. One of the most admired of his studies in this field is his examination of the development of the embryo in the egg. His method was simple but effective. Taking a gathering of eggs whose dates he could control he cut open an egg a day, so that he could observe the progress of development. Although there are obscurities in the text of his report there can be no serious difference of opinion about the matter of his discourse, for we can examine an egg for ourselves and need not fear that nature's arrangements in this sphere have changed much since Aristotle's day. The object of inquiry is here still before our eyes. The same is true of certain matters examined in the *Poetics*. *Catharsis* is either a figment of Aristotle's fancy or a variety of experience we too can examine. Varieties of experience are not so easily examined as an egg; we have nothing to put under a magnifying glass, and if we have to turn to psychologists, for such phenomena might be said to lie in their province, we shall perhaps get very diverse reports. *Catharsis*, however, is not a past event over and done with on which we can pronounce only after a careful examination of historical documents. Aristotle may have used the word in various senses; in the *Poetics* we can see to what its application is restricted. The question we have now to ask ourselves is this: Can we find a method more direct than those we have so far considered of studying the experience that Aristotle is describing when he says:

A tragedy is an imitation of an action . . . with incidents arousing pity and fear, wherewith to accomplish its *catharsis* of such emotions?

*Catharsis*, if a reality, must, like the egg, be very much today what it was in Aristotle's time. There remains only the difficulty of focusing our attention on it.

This focusing of the attention you may say offers a problem it may not be easy to solve to everyone's satisfaction. You will not be satisfied if I adopt the method called by the psychologists of my youth the Method of Introspection. Those with a thesis, even if they believe themselves to be seekers for the truth, may so easily deceive themselves, and it is difficult for the hearer to apply any adequate control to the evidence. I rule out, therefore, any personal testimony I might be able to offer; nor shall I ask you yourselves for the moment any leading questions that might be suspected of tendentiousness. Nor am I willing to go in the first instance to professional psychologists, for as I have suggested they may provide more perplexity than they remove. Modern psychologists have, however, examined aesthetic experience with an interest and understanding we may later profit by; but they come to the phenomena with working principles developed in another field. Freud, for example, long worked on a basis of two principles, the pleasure principle and the reality principle. Art he considered under the pleasure principle; it was he supposed a form of wish fulfilment, a kind of spiritual narcotic. So crude an analysis must not, however, cause one to overlook what may be helpful in his findings.

It is not then to psychologists but to those pioneers of the modern study of the mind, to the poets, that I wish to appeal in the first instance; to the Romantic poets and men of letters of that age who gave a new impetus to that inquiry into the self and especially into the workings of that part of the self now designated the imagination. Modern psychologists are their descendants in one branch of the family as it were, but they are a very junior branch and have much to learn before they can digest the discoveries of such inquirers as Wordsworth, Coleridge, Keats, and De Quincey. These men did not regard literature as belonging to a form of activity that was opposed to or divorced from reality. The assertions 'That Poetry is the breath and finer spirit of all knowledge' and that the Poet 'is the rock of defence of human nature' may seem rhetorical statements, but Wordsworth and those who followed him were able to give good reasons for such claims, and Freud's philosophy had not quite allowed for their significance. The poets and critics to whom I am going to appeal were men who had devoted themselves to the study of life and who raised thought on aesthetic problems once again to the level to which an analyst like Aristotle had brought it. Till the coming of the Romantics one need hardly look for any analytical discussion that will shed light on the phenomenon of *catharsis*. The Romantics, however, were as critical inquirers familiar with the experience.

To guard against doubtful testimony and to exclude, I trust, all disputable matter, I am adopting some rules for admissibility of evidence. The first is that the poet or critic must not be trying to explain Aristotle's words to us. This would rule out, did Milton come within our period, the explanation of *catharsis* prefixed to *Samson Agonistes*. I remind you of his views, however, that you may compare them with the observations of a later age:

Tragedy, as it was anciently composed, hath been ever held the gravest and most profitable of all other poems; therefore said by Aristotle to be of power, by raising pity and fear, or terror, to purge the mind of those and such like passions—that is, to temper and reduce them to just measure and a kind of delight, stirred up by reading or seeing those passions well imitated.

That is, I think, the best the Renaissance can do for us on *catharsis* from the critical angle. Yet it seems to me far from clear, and learned rather than lucid. Milton does not seem to me, though I recognize that many may feel differently, to see the matter with that inward sense that so illumines and clarifies his poetry.

My second rule, which is really a corollary to the first, is that the writer should be unaware he is talking of a phenomenon that has been called *catharsis*, yet that we should be able to recognize at once that he is referring to the variety of experience indicated by Aristotle.

This part of our inquiry is one in which those of you who are interested might help. I propose to examine with you now two passages that conform to the rules I have laid down for evidence, one briefly, the other at some length; later I shall cite other passages. Many of you, however, may think of even better instances of the unconscious elucidation of *catharsis*, and I shall be grateful for any references or suggestions you may care to offer me.

My first illustration is a very well known passage from Keats's letters:

The excellence of every art is its intensity, capable of

making all disagreeables evaporate, from their being in close relationship with Beauty and Truth. Examine *King Lear*, and you will find this exemplified throughout.

The Greek word κάθαρσις could be used of purification by fire. Keats has for the moment seen the experience in this light. The 'disagreeables' that evaporate may be equated with Aristotle's fear and pity. Galen refers to the painful and disquieting elements that are to be expelled as τὰ λυποῦντα; Keats's 'disagreeables' might serve as a translation of Galen's term.

Keats is for the moment speaking as a reader; we may regard the reader as sharing an experience that the author communicates to him. My next illustration shows the experience from the author's side and emphasizes what the author wishes to communicate. The author here is Keats's most influential teacher, Wordsworth, who comments at some length on the experience we wish to examine, and in his comment makes explicit what is regularly implicit in so much of his best prose and poetry.

In *Lyrical Ballads* of 1798 is the poem entitled *The Idiot Boy*. This, like *Simon Lee* in the same volume, has given occasion for a good deal of merriment at Wordsworth's expense. Soon after the First World War two young men published an anthology of what they regarded as among the world's worst poems. They included, I was told, *Simon Lee*. No one, however, who reads *Simon Lee* and its companions with the attention interest arouses can fail to see in them invaluable studies for later works that even the most critical recognize as excellent. The theme of *The Idiot Boy* is the relation of parent and child; Wordsworth is studying one of those great and simple affections of our nature that were to form the argument of his contribution to the *Ballads*. His purpose is most easily studied if we consider for a moment the doctrine from which he had just emancipated himself. His mentor, for a brief period, William Godwin had been for banishing the passions and affections in favour of political justice, and political justice forbad us to love our parents or our children merely because they were our parents or children. We should regard them (for love is too strong and unregulated a form of regard) on the same terms as all the world, and countenance them only in accordance with *their moral worth and their importance to the general weal*. It is doubtless true that parental affection is often of a mingled yarn. It may have strands of pride; sometimes, though not frequently in a civilized society, of hopes of gain. For I shall hardly be exaggerating if I say that most of the younger members of my audience can be written off by their parents even in our Welfare State as a total financial loss—yet their mothers are not likely to love them any the less. Wordsworth wishing to study the passion in its purity unsustained by any collateral supports makes the child of his poem an idiot that can quicken in the mother's heart no hopes of gain or worldly glory. To Godwin such a child could have no moral worth or importance to the general weal. The mother's love, therefore, is a free and natural expression of her own heart. Her love is in no way like political justice dependent on the apparent worth of the recipient. It is one of those unbought gifts of life that are specially dear at all times to the poets, however unreasonable they may seem to a mind of rationalistic bent. How dear to Wordsworth is clear from his reply to a critic of his poem.

Wordsworth's friend John Wilson (Christopher North) had written protesting against certain disagreeable features in the poem. The Idiot was in himself a displeasing sort of person, and nothing, argued Christopher North, is a fit subject for poetry that does not please. A similar objection had been raised against other of the *Ballads*, especially *Simon Lee*, whose swollen ankles had offended the feelings of some refined readers, as they sometimes do still; the ankles of a goddess are generally felt to be suitable for poetic comment, but those of a done old man, it was generally agreed, were not. Wordsworth's reply to these animadversions provides us with what I venture to regard as a classic account of the variety of experience Aristotle called *catharsis*.

The full force of Wordsworth's reply, however, is best felt if we have in mind not merely Christopher North's protest in 1802 but some observations on *The Idiot Boy* by Coleridge many years later. Coleridge thought that Wordsworth had not taken sufficient care to preclude from the reader's fancy the disgusting images of ordinary morbid idiocy; and he further objected

that the idiocy of the boy is so evenly balanced by the folly of the mother, as to present to the general reader rather a laughable burlesque on the blindness of anile dotage, than an analytic display of maternal affection in its ordinary workings.

Wordsworth begins his reply to Christopher North by asking who is to be the judge of what is pleasing. Men sometimes fail to find pleasure because of their ignorance or prejudice; and therefore the business of the poet as Wordsworth conceives it is not merely to reflect the feelings of human nature; the poet ought, Wordsworth feels, to travel before men occasionally as well as at their sides:

he ought, to a certain degree, to rectify men's feelings, to give them new compositions of feeling, to render their feelings more sane, pure, and permanent, in short, more consonant to nature, that is, to eternal nature, and the great moving spirit of things.

Wordsworth then goes on to consider the loathing and disgust which many people have at the sight of an idiot as a feeling which, though having some foundation in human nature, is not necessarily attached to it in any virtuous degree. Indeed such feelings seem to Wordsworth to show a certain want of comprehensiveness of thinking and feeling. Looking inward to his own thoughts he says:

I have often applied to idiots, in my own mind, that sublime expression of scripture that their life is hidden with God—

and then turning to the poem and its characters he tells us how he sees the conduct of the mother

as the great triumph of the human heart. It is there we see the strength, disinterestedness, and grandeur of love; nor have I ever been able to contemplate an object that calls out so many excellent and virtuous sentiments without finding it hallowed thereby, and having something in me which bears down before it, like a deluge, every feeble sensation of disgust and aversion.

If Keats described *catharsis* to us from the reader's side, this passage from Wordsworth lets us view it as the poet sees it. Keats uses the image of fire; Wordsworth that of the deluge; but the experience they describe is the same, and it is the experience to which Aristotle appealed in his refutation of Plato's charge that the poets and dramatists are the great corrupters of men. Wordsworth's analysis is not prompted directly as is that of Keats by some tragic action of the scope of *King Lear*; but he is contemplating the elements of our nature that are found compounded in tragedy, and his examination of the properties of these elements is the simplest and surest approach to our understanding of Shakespeare's profoundly studied syntheses.

The passages from Keats and Wordsworth are offered as admissible evidence, for neither poet had Aristotle in mind. Wordsworth in the enlarged *Preface* of 1802 says: 'Aristotle, I have been told, hath said that Poetry is the most philosophic of all writing'—Wordsworth was not, then, at the time he was writing to Christopher North a student of the *Poetics*. I am not aware of any evidence that would show that Keats was one either. Later I shall have occasion to draw your attention to other accounts of the phenomenon, including one by Lessing, but as Lessing was a most scholarly reader of the *Poetics* what he says is not at present evidence. I should be glad to add to my collection of such passages and I hope some of my listeners will help me. I am aware, however, that *Hyperion* and its revision both treat of *catharsis*.

That both Keats and Wordsworth are describing the variety of experience Aristotle had in mind is clear, I think, not merely because we have the 'disagreeables', to use Keats's word, disposed of by fire or deluge, but because the experience as described by the poets refutes Plato's charge against Homer and his descendants, that they encourage the weaker side of our nature. Any acceptable account of *catharsis* must satisfy this condition, for on the experience Aristotle built his reply to Plato. The effect Aristotle attributes implicitly to the experience is made fully explicit in the account by Keats and especially in Wordsworth's. Keats emphasizes Beauty and Truth as the elements producing the intensity that disposes of the disagreeables; Wordsworth talks of rendering our feelings more sane, pure, and permanent; our eye is directed to the strength, disinterestedness, and grandeur, of one of the primary affections. Plato could hardly have taken exception to a type of experience that left men so fortified, whatever his feelings might have been about the artistry of the *Ballads*; for what the great Romantics are insisting on is that poetic experience points to a wise and manly path in life, the way required of us by Plato. Naturally we wish to be as manful as the man of stone that Housman came on in the Grecian gallery; but we have to work in a different material from marble. To feel and yet to endure is an art beyond the virtue of stone; living at its best demands the art of reconciling apparent opposites that Pericles praised as the glory of the Athenian way of life. *Catharsis* is as it were a window on such an ideal, for through it what has appeared the weakness of man is seen to be strength. That is why Aristotle found in this variety of experience the complete justification of art.

In the problem we are investigating the poets and men of letters must always be our principal witnesses; but I turn now, though not for long, to a psychologist—to Freud. Till late in life Freud had worked on the assumption that dreams were a form of wish-fulfilment. We are asleep, but something in our minds is about to disturb our slumbers; fortunately there is a mechanism to lull this disturber into quiescence by beguiling it with what on waking we call a dream. Freud, however, discovered that there are dreams that do not seem to offer a wish-fulfilment. Men fight over again in sleep the desperate encounters from which they may have come away maimed and wounded. Here, to adopt the words of Professor Trilling in his brilliant study of Freud's doctrine in its relation to art, the mind seems in such terrible dreams to be embracing its own pain for some vital purpose; and Professor Trilling goes on to suggest that had Freud applied his new findings about such dreams to art he would have seen that in tragedy also the mind confronts pain for some vital purpose. The relegation of art to the class of wish-fulfillers was an error that should have been abandoned by Freud when he revised his classification of dreams. Accordingly Professor Trilling very reasonably argues that just as in fearful dreams the suffering patient seems to be struggling to gain a mastery impossible in mere passive experience, so in tragedy the dramatist and the spectator fight for a similar victory. With this analogy in mind Professor Trilling concludes that

the cathartic theory of tragedy as usually understood inadequately suggests the sense of active mastery.

What 'the cathartic theory of tragedy as usually understood' tells us we need not pause to inquire; for I shall plead that the account of *catharsis* found in Keats and Wordsworth stresses above all else precisely this sense of active mastery required by Professor Trilling. There is no turning aside from the fearful elements of existence; the disagreeables have to be mastered in the intensity of the encounter.

For the moment I am not concerned with the truth or otherwise of Freud's doctrines. I merely wish to remind you of the demand one of Freud's most persuasive interpreters makes of any formulation of *catharsis* that he can accept as adequate; and to claim that the account given by Keats and Wordsworth meets that demand completely. As far as I understand the position these poets stand on what may be called firm psychological ground. This is not surprising, for the poets are to the manner born in a region where psychologists have been as Freud himself acknowledged only recently naturalized.

We are now in a position to ask if this variety of experience we know as *catharsis* is induced only by tragedies in which the protagonist exhibits what is called a tragic flaw. There seems nothing in the nature of the experience itself to require such an assumption. Calamity and suffering are elements in tragedy; but does a man's bringing these on himself by folly or wickedness make his situation more tragic than that of the man who perishes for some loyalty or duty or sense of honour? Wordsworth's analysis of the experience might be taken as proving that the essential feature on which the mind finally rests is some positive virtue that kindles the intensity of conviction that is the essence of the experience. Such a virtue may be found as Wordsworth himself explains even in wicked men:

> For, strength to persevere and to support
> And energy to conquer and repel—

These elements of virtue, that declare
The native grandeur of the human soul—
Are ofttimes not unprofitably shown
In the perverseness of a selfish course.

The bad man, if we may use so simple an expression, attains the dignity of a tragic hero only by the possession of 'those elements of virtue' in him that we must acknowledge and admire.

Perhaps then it is no disloyalty to Bradley to untwist one of the strands entangled in his views on tragedy. Bradley, in describing the tendency of the protagonist to identify his whole being with some interest, or object, as a gift of greatness, is pointing to the true nature of tragedy. Without this concentration the elements of virtue in the hero or villain could not be raised to that intensity in which the excellence of the work consists. That it is the elements of virtue that provide the intensity is recognized by Bradley when he talks of the tragic hero as in some sense superior to the world. As it is this sense of superiority or triumph that seems to obliterate all other considerations, we may fairly argue that Bradley, in spite of his attempt to treat *hamartia* as the central fact in tragedy, does realize that it takes its character and significance not from faults but from virtues.

I cannot now admit that the producer is entitled to

cite Bradley in support of the idea of *Hamlet* set out in the Prologue to the film. Bradley has doubtless expounded at length the doctrine of the tragic flaw but with such qualifications as, I maintain, discredit his evidence. Indeed, I hope eventually, on the strength of his feeling that the tragic hero is undone by his very virtues, to treat him as a witness for the prosecution rather than the defence. Even allowing, you may now say to me, that Bradley may for the moment be put aside as a doubtful witness, there still remain for examination not only Aristotle but those even more authoritative witnesses the Greek tragedians themselves—the men who invented the literary form we call tragedy. Show us that they too based tragedy not on men's faults but on their virtues and we shall give up Bradley also. Meantime, however, we challenge you to explain away Aristotle's explicit statement about the tragic flaw and must ask you to offer the reinterpretation of the vision of the great tragedians that your denial of the doctrine of *hamartia* demands.

# III

## THE HEROIC TRADITION

AFTER considering the charge against Bradley that he is not a whole-hearted adherent to the doctrine of *hamartia*, we agreed that there was reason in the accusation, but instead of convicting him of inconsistency we congratulated him, if I may say so, on seeing that the doctrine, which he had set himself so determinedly to expound to us, was inadequate to account for our reactions to the impact of tragedy. Bradley, had he first examined the phenomenon of *catharsis*—to which *hamartia* is quite secondary—would have seen, so we suggested, that the qualifications he had later to add to his exposition of the tragic flaw should not have been given second place in a kind of footnote but treated as the leading principle, a principle in whose train the virtues follow of course, and the faults by accident. But how, you asked, can any such argument be maintained in face of Aristotle's plain avowal of his contrary opinion? Aristotle was the first to draw attention, as far as we know, to the phenomenon of *catharsis* in aesthetic experience; Aristotle is no less the originator of the explanation found in *hamartia*. Am I going to be so paradoxical, you may ask, as to argue that Aristotle is, like Bradley, not a whole-hearted expositor of his own suggestion? Where can we find any hint that Aristotle felt the doctrine of *hamartia* inadequate as an explanation of *catharsis*?

If we confine ourselves to the *Poetics* we shall not find any retraction or qualification of the doctrine of *hamartia*; but the *Poetics* whatever it is, whether Aristotle's notes or those of a pupil, was not published by its author. The story of how the works that we have by Aristotle survived is a strange one: almost all that he published has perished; it is his lecture notes that remain to us as in the *Ethics*. These facts, hardly allowed for adequately in the traditional criticism of Aristotle, have, on further consideration, led to what may fairly be called a new approach to his work. Even in a philosopher's published work we may expect to find developments or shifts of emphasis or even a revision or recantation of views once maintained. That is why it is so important to have, in the study of Plato for instance, a chronological basis on which to work. If this is true of published work, how much more necessary is it to allow for similar modifications in a lecturer's working notes, especially in those of one so eminently capable of development as Aristotle, who, though an original mind, spent twenty years as the pupil of an equally eminent and original teacher, a teacher, however, with a very different bent from that of his pupil. Commentators today, therefore, following Professor Werner Jaeger's lead, are not so disturbed as former critics by changes of emphasis in what we have of Aristotle's lectures; the commentators no longer strive to reconcile the contradictory in the lectures by some logical argument, nor do they reject as spurious those writings that cannot at first sight be squared with what seem Aristotle's maturest findings. It has become part of the business of the student of Aristotle, as it has long been the business of students of other great minds, to plot the curve, we may say, of their subject's development; in short to regard the work not statically but dynamically.

We must keep in mind not merely the circumstances in which the *Poetics* has come down to us; we must remember the facts that provided the occasion for the delivery of the lectures. Plato had in the *Republic* denounced the tragic artists and their master Homer as propagators of unethical doctrine; the poets entertained their delighted but misguided readers or spectators with bad examples. The theatre, Plato had argued, shows us a succession of characters cursing the spite that had inflicted on them their grievous lot and crying out against their fate, when they should have been keeping, in the

Scots phrase, a calm sough, or, as the once popular
English expression put it, a stiff upper lip. Men,
Plato contended, must, if they are to be worthy of
the name, oppose a firm front to adversity, and
instead of venting their pain and grief on their
fellows consume their own smoke. With this ideal
the dramatists are careful, Plato suggests, to have
nothing to do; for such an ideal of character would
give no scope for the declamations and tirades that
delight an audience; there would be no opportunity
for indulging the spectators in the fear and pity that
men are only too ready to give way to. The dramatists of necessity select a type of character that cannot
be regarded as a model for the ideal citizen. The
poets must be expelled, however politely, from the
ideal state.

The *Poetics* has to meet these objections by Plato.
From the beginning Aristotle makes it clear that
there will be no attempt to minimize the emotional
excitement that the dramatists must rouse if they are
to be successful; but by a wonderful stroke of genius
and insight Aristotle turns this emotional experience
into the very justification of the dramatist's art. By
indicating the peculiar variety of experience the
tragic artist induces, Aristotle can claim that the
dramatist far from producing a relaxed and merely
enervated condition in his audience has left them

with a faith in life that rises superior to the accidents of our lot, however natural it may be to feel in the first instance the pity and fear that calamity begets. All this is, by general consent, implied in Aristotle's reference to *catharsis*. He himself puts the matter briefly, but the context in which his argument obviously stands, namely Plato's criticism of the poets, makes any other interpretation meaningless. Further, we find in Keats and Wordsworth, and indeed elsewhere too, evidence that confirms in detail this interpretation of Aristotle's meaning. Aristotle is the first critic to offer the rational inquirer a satisfactory justification of what appears our most irrational satisfaction in tragic drama. Why then should we hesitate to accept his further views on the tragic flaw?

We are entitled to reconsider Aristotle's notion of the tragic flaw, if we find it incompatible with his central idea of the nature of tragedy. The indispensable features of the form we have been able to study for ourselves. What Aristotle called *catharsis* is still as available for examination as in the fourth century before Christ. The examination we have so far been able to make does not suggest that a tragic flaw is a pre-condition of the phenomenon. It is true, as was admitted earlier, that this phenomenon is more difficult to examine than an egg, and that we are bound to look for confirmation or contradiction of our findings with some care. If, however, it could be shown that Aristotle not only failed in the *Poetics* to establish his contention about the tragic flaw but elsewhere decisively rejected the notion, he might then be put with Bradley as one whose evidence about the tragic flaw may be regarded as doubtful.

Aristotle in the *Poetics* in support of his notion of *hamartia* commits himself to the statement that a plot in which a good man passes from happiness to misery is not fear-inspiring but simply odious. This is an essential link in his argument, and if it does not hold the general contention falls in pieces. Even if we put aside the fate of the saints and the martyrs as inspiring only to Christians, surely Plato had made the death of Socrates as nearly a form of martyrdom as we can ask; further, to free Aristotle from all criticism on this count, we should have to insist on what is very doubtful, namely that the Greek dramatists never show us the good man suffering an unhappy fate. For, taking Aristotle at his word, we must conclude that the hero of a proper tragedy cannot be without some fault. Nor need there be, as some have argued, any doubt that the fault must be not merely an error of judgement but a moral fault. If the hero cannot be entirely good without his downfall giving us offence, surely this implies that the

fault must be of a moral kind. The manner in which
Aristotle links the doctrine of *hamartia* with the
phenomenon of *catharsis* confirms this:

The first situation [that is one in which a good man
passes from happiness to misery] is not fear-inspiring or
piteous, but simply odious to us.

Such goodness would exclude, so Aristotle argues,
fear and pity, and these are essential to *catharsis*.

If it were now objected that the distinctions
Aristotle makes in his argument about the 'good'
man and his place in tragedy are too fine to be summarized in this coarse and perhaps tendentious style,
and that these distinctions cannot be treated except
at length and in the most thorough and scholarly
manner, we can only reply that there is fortunately
other evidence concerning Aristotle's own personal
feelings about such a situation that makes the detailed argument about his views in this section of the
*Poetics* of what is called academic interest. Aristotle
was to experience in the fortunes of a friend an
affair that can only be described as odious, and we
have a record of Aristotle's reactions to the event.

On the death of Plato, Aristotle left the Academy
and went to Asia Minor, settling in the territory of
Hermeias who had his centre of government at
Atarneus. Hermeias had already given hospitality
to men associated with the Academy; it is clear he

gave a special welcome to Aristotle, for Hermeias, although a ruler who had gained and maintained his authority not by philosophic meditation but by force of arms, cherished the ideal of subordinating force to a wisdom and conduct that could be called humane. He was unfortunately between two mighty opposites: on one side the Persians, on the other the rapidly maturing Macedon. In spite of his experience Hermeias took a risk that allowed the Persians to lay treacherous hands on him, and his death by torture was the sequel; for Hermeias would not disclose his knowledge of Macedon's intentions. Aristotle was particularly affected by the tragic end of his friend, for he must have known him well and indeed soon after married his niece. Aristotle like other members of the Academy had honoured Hermeias for his liberal and humane ideals, and now in his adversity Hermeias had conducted himself in what Aristotle felt was a truly heroic fashion. It is this mingling of affection and admiration that finds expression in the lines Aristotle wrote in memory of the dead ruler, the lines on *Virtue* that begin,

> Virtue toilsome to mortal race,
> Fairest prize in life.

'Virtue' is here used to translate the Greek ἀρετή, for our scholarly instructors, although they sometimes say that the Greek is never to be so translated,

often find that no other word than *virtue* will serve.
Here *virtue*, however inadequate an equivalent, is
near enough for our present purpose, although I
shall sometimes use the form *areté* in its place. The
prize then that Hermeias has won is that immortal
*areté*, the prize for which, the poem tells us, the heroes
of old, Ajax and Achilles, reckoned death a cheap
price. For that prize they did not hesitate to go to
the halls of death. Because of this love of Virtue they
are forever famous in song; this fame Hermeias now
shares with them.

Aristotle makes no reference in the poem to any
form of *hamartia* that might render the death of
Hermeias less odious; although the comparison
between the conduct of his friend and that of Ajax
and Achilles could, it might be thought, have provided a philosopher with an excuse for the mention
of faults. In her animadversions on Bradley Professor Campbell was critical, you may remember, of
the notion that the tragic flaw seemed from some
points of view the source of the hero's greatness, and
she cited in support of her condemnation of Bradley
the *Ajax* of Sophocles where, she argued, the man's
unheroic and intemperate anger undid all his good
and greatness. Aristotle seems to have felt differently about Ajax, when he found in him the ideal
that Hermeias had not failed to live up to. It is clear

that what Aristotle told his students in his lectures was now quite inadequate to express his passionate admiration for the heroic ideal as he found it in life, and he felt for his friend what he now realized the poets had felt for the virtue they embodied in Ajax and Achilles.

No thought of flaw or fault could have strengthened Aristotle's sense of his friend's heroism or have made less odious for the philosopher the murder of this enlightened ruler. The only redeeming feature in the terrible story was the courage and loyalty of Hermeias. We may fairly ask the question why the sense of redemption or reconciliation induced by the tragic drama demands a factor not required in life itself. To attempt some distinction between life and art in this particular that will explain such a discrepancy is to ignore Aristotle's own insistence on their congruence, for how otherwise should he appeal on his friend's behalf from life to literature. As Aristotle appealed to the poets to confirm his own convictions and experience, so we in turn may appeal to Aristotle's own experience when we consider his interpretation of the poets. What consumes or sweeps away the disagreeables is not some nice calculation arrived at by weighing the hero's fate against the faults and mistakes that are inseparable from mortality but the sense of something in mortals that has risen superior to their condition. In this Aristotle, as his tribute to Hermeias proves, is at one with Keats and Wordsworth.

In his most learned and exhaustive study of certain elements in Greek education and culture, Professor Jaeger has cited Aristotle's poem as one of the many testimonies to the truth of the thesis that

The Homeric poems and the great Athenian philosophers are bound together by the continuing life of the old Hellenic ideal of areté.

In his effort to do justice to the memory of his friend, Aristotle in the fourth century reaches out for his comparisons to Homer and to the tragic dramatists of the fifth century, for the tragic poets of that age were the real Homeridae, the true sons of Homer. Nor does Plato's rejection of Homer and the poets run counter to Professor Jaeger's argument. Plato does not reject the *areté* they glorify, and no one quotes more aptly and nobly from Homer to justify his own conception of *areté* than Plato. Aristotle's lines on Hermeias entitle us not only to question Aristotle's own treatment of the doctrine of *hamartia*; they suggest a further question about the traditional interpretation of the Greek dramatists that is based on this doctrine. Are the Greek dramatists, as Aristotle's reference to Ajax seems to suggest, and as Professor Jaeger argues with the force of a massive scholarship, inspired not by their scrutiny of the faults and failings of men but by a sense of their virtues?

I can now imagine your saying to me—Even if it could be shown from a single poem and from the seventh book of the *Ethics* that Aristotle really regarded the Tragedies of the·fifth century as a glorification of the virtues of men and women rather than as examples of human frailty leading to disaster—even if this were admitted for argument's sake, what of the dramatists themselves? They have regularly been expounded to us in terms of the doctrine of *hamartia*. Do you reject this as inadequate and untrue to the spirit in which their authors looked on the life of man? Can you deny that the moral prudence taught in chorus and iambic stresses the faults and flaws of humanity? Do you refuse to believe that Antigone was undutifully stubborn, or Ajax unjustifiably proud, or Oedipus wilfully rash and violent? In short, am I prepared to argue that it was their virtues and not their vices that brought them to disaster—that in the words of Aristotle it was for love of virtue that the tragic heroes went to the halls of death?

Fortunately it requires no great courage to say yes to these questions; for, following the line of thought that has just been indicated as taken by

Jaeger, there are scholars who have come to regard the dramatists of the fifth century as the exponents of a heroic ideal and not as judges who summon to their tribunal the great spirits of antiquity only to convict them of some fault that justifies the gods in having visited on them their tragic fate. It is not here possible to treat of this topic at length; nor do I speak with the authority that would entitle me to do so; yet I must touch, however briefly and imperfectly, on the Greek drama, for, though my argument could stand without this collateral testimony, the evidence I shall elicit from this source may incline you to give more heed to my story.

Taking advantage of Mr. Wolfit's *Oedipus* productions running at Hammersmith, I shall confine my remarks for brevity's sake to Sophocles, especially as these productions have drawn from distinguished dramatic critics observations that may enable you to understand why what I have to say, although it may seem too simple and obvious to be worth saying, is still necessary, if we are to look fairly at the literary form which Aeschylus and Sophocles created. Further, I shall have the excuse of recommending you to read Professor Whitman's *Sophocles*, which has not yet had the notice in this country I am sure it deserves. What he has said about Sophocles and what I shall venture to say about Shakespeare so agree that you may, if only because of the coincidence, think my conclusion worth pondering. The accident that has suggested Sophocles as the representative of the ancient tradition need not fortunately lead to any distortion or partiality in the argument, for scholars are agreed that it was the tragedies of Sophocles, particularly his *Oedipus*, that suggested to Aristotle his observations on the tragic hero. It will not be unfair, therefore, if we ask if the doctrine of *hamartia* makes sense of Sophocles.

Let us look at the plot of the *Oedipus* for ourselves. Before the action opens Oedipus, as we learn in the course of the play, has slain his father and married his mother. As it was in his very zeal to avoid these disasters that he brought them about, he can hardly be held guilty on that score. But his subsequent conduct, you may say, his impetuosity, his fiery insistence on sifting the evidence to the last iota, a ruthlessness that drives his wife and mother to her death, and leaves such a feeling of guilt that he must blind himself to expiate his deeds—are not these facts sufficient to justify our talking of a flaw in this otherwise good and wise man? Of Oedipus as of other tragic protagonists may we not say with one commentator whose word may here stand for many of a like mind:

There has generally been some fault—some hastiness or pride or excess of confidence, some breach of αἰδώς or σωφροσύνη, which makes the suffering, if not deserved, yet explicable, and not wholly inappropriate?

Yet it is this kind of interpretation of Sophocles that drew from Mr. Ivor Brown, in his notice, in last Sunday's *Observer* (8 February 1953), of Mr. Wolfit's performance of Oedipus, a denunciation of the dramatist that I feel we must consider. Mr. Ivor Brown rejects the accusation that the conduct of Oedipus is worthy of blame or punishment, for what is he but a slave of destiny, a puppet with whom the gods deliberately sport? 'Yet', continues Mr. Brown,

Yet, because Greek tragedy was part of a religious ritual and far closer to a church service than to our box-office theatre, the well-behaved dramatists had to maintain that these gross injustices were all divinely right and proper. Says the chorus, 'Phoebus our Lord, be this according to thy will'. Sophocles was no probing philosopher, and certainly no rebel. He did a conservative's noble best for the repulsive, and even absurd, myth.

Mr. Ivor Brown's castigation of Sophocles comes from his assumption that Sophocles is, to borrow Mr. E. M. Forster's words, a kind of enlightened bishop. The assumption is doubtless somewhat hard on the bishops: on Sophocles it is, as Mr. Forster implies, little less than a libel. Sophocles had no such

pretensions as Mr. Brown imputes to him; for why
should the Chorus not express a view that is dramatic in the sense that it is to be interpreted in the
context of the action as a whole? In *King Lear*
Gloster says,

> As flies to wanton boys are we to the gods;
> They kill us for their sport.

But critics of any discernment have long ago given
up treating this as the key to Shakespeare's intention. May not Mr. Ivor Brown be thrusting on
Sophocles a sentiment natural perhaps to the Chorus
in its sudden but false hope that Oedipus will be
vindicated in his search for the secret of his ancestry,
a sentiment and a hope, however, that Sophocles
uses to make us feel the force of the despair that
follows?

All this granted, there still remains, you may say,
Mr. Ivor Brown's aversion from what he calls the
repulsive and absurd myth; for in his aversion he is
by no means singular and shares the antipathies
particularly of one who might well have been a
bishop, had not this churchman's reproofs to what
he considered the Erastianism of his countrymen
seemed to the government of his day somewhat
unenlightened. Keble, however, though he never
ascended an episcopal throne, exercised from the
Chair of Poetry, which Oxford was happy to reserve

for him for many years, an authority that still must command our respect, although readers of his discourse with a Newman's appreciation of the colour and bouquet of its Latinity have not become more numerous. At Oxford Keble had no need to keep in step with those leading the march-of-mind in his generation and could pause to look back on the journey so far achieved by the human spirit, and especially on those episodes in the venture where the poets of antiquity had revealed their prowess or skill. In this story Sophocles would play, one might have thought, a heroic part, and his almost notorious piety have gained the heart of a historian who would, it has been said, extract 'from Homer's almost savage animism the full grown mysteries of the Christian faith'. Yet to our astonishment Keble has as little admiration as Mr. Ivor Brown for Sophocles; here is what he says of the *Oedipus*:

the details of the story are so shocking; indeed to confess the truth, it has always seemed to me to border on that class of story which Aristotle himself rejects as being monstrous and repulsive, and it goes against our right feeling that one who is innocent of any crime should be so harshly punished, and should leave the stage without hope, without even an implied suggestion that at some future time his fate may take a happier turn: just as if some relentless genie played with men's fortunes as with dice.

And Keble finally passes judgement on Sophocles as a man 'without true religious feeling, without pity'. Mr. Ivor Brown's indictment goes only this much farther that for him the lack of true religious feeling is aggravated by an assumption of piety.

As to the myth being repulsive and absurd, if taken by itself and quite apart from the use Sophocles makes of it, I have nothing to say except that I shared that feeling when I first encountered what may be called a non-fictional reference to the marriage of parent and child. When I first crossed the border and at length stood in an Anglican church I was astonished to see displayed on one side of the altar the ten commandments, for I had supposed they were too well committed to everyone's memory to make such publication necessary; but this astonishment was nothing to the horror with which I read on the other hand a series of prohibitions beginning: 'A man may not marry his grandmother.' To hint at such possibilities seemed outrageous. Since then we have all been told that the reactions I describe are part of the evidence of guilt, and if this were indeed true one could not consider the complex too seriously nor could one dismiss the myth merely because it seemed repulsive. Truth unconditional and honest must be our aim. Our immediate business, however, is with the use Sophocles has made of the myth.

In what follows I shall venture to argue that both the contemporary critic and the former Professor of Poetry have misrepresented Sophocles to us, though for different reasons. Mr. Ivor Brown seems to accept what may be called the orthodox view of Sophocles, as a dramatist whose purpose is to justify the ways of the gods to men; to clear the gods Sophocles must convict the mortals themselves as the authors of their proper woe; finding that what he has been offered as pious assurances are no more than shameless and unfeeling platitudes, Mr. Ivor Brown turns on Sophocles instead of questioning the commentators. Keble, in contrast, was never so indoctrinated; he saw for himself that this story of the pious pleader for the gods is not dramatically written in the text; and not finding the piety there, only what seemed a stark delineation of the horrors of life, Keble could not feel, any more than many can feel in *King Lear*, a true religious feeling. The *Oedipus*, it must be admitted, is as difficult a play to interpret as *King Lear*; and who, you may ask, has a right to challenge the readings of Keble or Mr. Ivor Brown? Fortunately Sophocles took up once again the story of Oedipus and completed it in his last play of all, the *Oedipus at Colonus*. Here there can be little argument about the dramatist's purpose, and we may use the light we find here to help us to look back into the earlier and obscurer work.

Oedipus, in his old age, has been driven out of Thebes by Creon; his sons have made no move to help him, although they are now grown to powerful manhood; his daughters alone assist their father. The play opens with Antigone leading in the blind and miserably clad father and seating him on a stone in the shelter of a restful grove. A man of Colonus now enters and is troubled at the sight of so miserable a stranger seated in the grove sacred to the Eumenides. Oedipus on learning where he rests now knows he has reached the end appointed him by the gods, and he asks the man of Colonus to send for Theseus who as ruler of Athens governs at Colonus. The man departs, and the Chorus of elders from Colonus enter, warned of an intruder's presence by the countryman that had first encountered Oedipus. They are horrified to find the sacred place polluted by one who seems so unblest by the gods, and they insist on his coming from the sacred precincts and speaking to them on less forbidden ground. Finally when they learn who he is they are horrified at his very presence in Attica and desire him to quit their soil immediately. Theseus, however, when he arrives, is, quite unlike the Chorus, in no way frightened by superstitious fears of pollution;

learning the plight in which Oedipus finds himself, Theseus promises that Athens will protect him when alive, and give him the rights of burial he craves when his time comes to die. Theseus has no difficulty in looking through the externals of his guest's condition and realizing the truth in the claim by Oedipus that he has come to make Athens a gift of his bones and to work from his tomb for the salvation of the land.

Two points of view are contrasted in this and subsequent scenes: on the one side are the timid and conventional Chorus fearful that the presence of one on whom the gods have heaped so many misfortunes will only bring misfortune to those who befriend him. And this superstition becomes even more hateful in the Thebans who now come on the scene to lead Oedipus back to Thebes, by force or guile. For they have learnt that the presence of Oedipus will be of service to them; although they regard him as a polluted man and have no intention of receiving him as a free member of their community, they are prepared to use him merely as a tool in their designs.

With this we compare the attitude that Oedipus maintains towards himself and its acceptance by Theseus. Oedipus has come to institute a cult because he knows he is a heroic figure; from the grave of the hero, there came, as all believed, a virtue that quickens the living; for Oedipus rejects utterly the idea that he is a guilty man. His conduct has not been that of a guilty man, but of a hero. In his great reply to what he describes as the impious charges of Creon, he goes over his terrible story point by point and refuses to admit even the shadow of a fault. He is assured of his own integrity. And should you ask what further evidence there is of his claim, you have its full acceptance by the heroic Theseus and its confirmation, at the close, by heaven itself.

No doubt the *Oedipus at Colonus* requires for its detailed interpretation an extensive historical knowledge. We need perhaps to know something of the cult of the heroic dead throughout Greece, of the relations between Thebes and Athens at the time Sophocles was writing the play, and other such detail. But there is a larger historical setting too in which we may consider the work, and it is this setting that determines the path on which we must approach its significance. The fifth century saw at Athens a change in the moral outlook of mankind—or rather a development. It now became possible for men to believe that outward misery and distress were not necessarily proof of inward guilt. Such an enlightenment was not confined to Athens. It is, of course, the culmination of Hebrew prophecy and finds its embodiment there in the figure of the suffering servant.

The Hebrew genius unlike the Greek did not find expression in dramatic form; but the work in their literature that approaches most nearly to the drama is the *Book of Job*, and, like the *Oedipus at Colonus*, the *Book of Job* presents to us a figure who asserts, in spite of all the testimony outward conditions seem to bear against him, that he is free from guilt, that his calamities are not the consequence of his actions.

Job might be speaking for Oedipus as he says:

He hath stripped me of my glory and taken the crown from my head.

He hath put my brethren far from me and mine acquaintance are verily estranged from me.

Like Oedipus Job is in rags and an outcast, but like Oedipus he never wavers and his faith is enshrined in the famous lines:

For I know that my redeemer liveth.

These words have since received an amplification in the mind of mankind that, however relevant, is not for the moment at issue. What is immediately relevant is that the words of Job, taken in their dramatic context, express the very heart of the faith of Oedipus. *His* plea, like that of Job, is against the material assessment that the world can hardly refrain from adopting. And Sophocles, like the author of the *Book of Job*, adapts his story to express his belief that the root of the matter, to borrow the words of Job, is found in Oedipus. To Job God speaks from heaven, and to Eliphaz the Temanite and his friends he says:

My wrath is kindled against thee, and against thy two friends: for ye have not spoken of me the thing that is right as my servant Job hath.

In the *Oedipus at Colonus* the Greek dramatist uses his own but analogous symbols to obtain the same effect. The peals of thunder from heaven announce the completion of the hero's pilgrimage; he sends for Theseus and, although blind, leads the way into the sacred grove and there, having taken farewell of his daughters, he goes accompanied only by Theseus to his deification.

Sophocles is as objective an artist as Shakespeare; but as men draw towards their end they care less, as Newman observes of his own *Apologia*, for disclosures. In his last works Sophocles, like Shakespeare in his, seems to turn back on himself to offer in a more explicit form the vision that it has been his purpose to embody in his works; and to do so he has to have recourse to a symbolism that can be misunderstood apart from its context. It is so also in the *Book of Job*; you can say that God has treated Job like a puppet, and that to slaughter his children as a test of his faith is a crime for which there can be no atonement.

To give him more sons and daughters can be no compensation whatever. Yet no one would think of taking the *Book of Job* as an indictment of God or regard its author, on the other hand, as some conservative apologist for a tyrannical Immortal. The *Book of Job* is a vindication of Job from the material judgement of the world—it is an affirmation of a faith in righteousness whatever the event. The affirmation that provides the inspiration of the *Oedipus at Colonus* is of the same kind. The man whom the gods have seemed to reject is vindicated. Sophocles no more than the author of the *Book of Job* stands forth as an accuser of the gods, or as an apologist for cruelty and tyranny. It is enough for him to have vindicated the heroic spirit and in spite of the superstition and the blind selfishness of the world to have made manifest on which side his heart is to be found. This was the inspiration of the *Oedipus* no less than that of the *Oedipus at Colonus*, but it is only at the end that the poet in the charity of his last years condescends to make explicit to us what we should have known was implicit from the first.

I have cited the *Oedipus at Colonus* as the testimony provided by Sophocles himself that any doctrine of *hamartia* makes nonsense of his purpose. To say that the sufferings of Oedipus or Job are, if not deserved, yet explicable, and not wholly inappropriate, is a mere perversion of the evidence, unless you add that suffering that leads to deification or draws commendation from heaven would be appropriate to us all.

Having cited the *Oedipus at Colonus* to dispose of the idea that Sophocles built his drama round some tragic flaw that thereby he might put on the shoulders of men the guilt of the gods, I turn to the play immediately preceding his last, to the *Philoctetes*, to illustrate the cathartic power of his vision, and to emphasize through this illustration that the experience we call *catharsis* is quite independent of all the considerations suggested by *hamartia*.

Philoctetes on the way to the siege of Troy lands with the other Greeks to sacrifice at an island shrine and is bitten in the foot by a snake that guards the holy place. So horrible is the nature of the wound, and so terrible the victim's sufferings, that the Greek leaders, unable to endure his cries of agony and the stench of the suppurating flesh, and regarding the afflicted man as a polluted being whose presence would render all sacrifice vain, contrive to abandon him on the island of Lemnos. There he languishes in solitude and pain saved only by the possession of his wonderful bow which never misses and whose arrows carry instant death. This bow Hercules had

given him as a reward for lighting the pyre which
was to deliver the hero from the torments of the
shirt of Nessus. When the play begins ten years
have passed since Philoctetes was doomed to solitude, and at Troy Achilles has fallen, and Ajax has
killed himself when the arms of Achilles were
adjudged to Odysseus; the Greeks, however, have
now discovered in their despair that they cannot
capture Troy till they bring to their camp the son of
Achilles and with him Philoctetes and his magic bow.

The play opens with Odysseus and Neoptolemus
landing on Lemnos, for Odysseus has promised to
bring to Troy the men whose presence is needed for
victory, and he has first collected Neoptolemus. Now
Odysseus explains to Neoptolemus how they must
conduct themselves if they are to make sure of
Philoctetes. Odysseus dare not show himself to
Philoctetes, for, as he explains, the lonely man
would vent his anger on one whom he regarded as
a chief betrayer; nor is it any good inviting Philoctetes to go to Troy so deep is his hatred of Aga-
memnon and Menelaus. Neoptolemus must pretend
he is on his way home from Troy, having quarrelled
with the leaders who gave his father's arms to
Odysseus; he must offer to take Philoctetes home
with him. Once aboard ship, however, they can tell
another tale. Neoptolemus protests against such

trickery; he is for using force or abandoning the task; he is, however, finally won over.

Neoptolemus quickly gains the confidence of the lonely man who inquires anxiously for his comrades at Troy only to learn that those he respected are dead and that it is the villains who survive; as they are about to leave for the ship the wound becomes overpoweringly painful, and Philoctetes falls into an exhausted slumber, having confided his bow to Neoptolemus. Neoptolemus, as soon as Philoctetes recovers, feels bound to confess the deception he is practising on him, and is so moved by the reproaches this calls forth that he would restore the bow, did not Odysseus suddenly appear from hiding and carry it off. Philoctetes is now confronted with the alternatives of following the bow to the ship or remaining behind quite helpless and doomed to certain death. He does not, however, hesitate: death is preferable to submission to such inhuman tricksters. The Chorus try to persuade him that he is the author of his own woe. He can choose to save his life if he cares. Such a choice Philoctetes regards as impossible. Just as he contemplates suicide Neoptolemus arrives with the bow and in spite of all Odysseus can do restores it to its owner. Odysseus has to take himself off hastily. Neoptolemus now puts it to Philoctetes that having regained his bow he can come of his own free will to Troy and that there he will be cured of his wound as the seer foretells and, in addition, gain immortal glory as the conqueror of Troy. But just as the prospect of death could not move Philoctetes, so now the promise of healing and of glory leaves his resolution unshaken. He will not go to Troy, and he now calls upon Neoptolemus to make good his promise to take him home. They are about to go when Hercules appears before them—to forbid them to return to Greece. He himself, the god reminds them, has won immortal glory by his many and great labours. 'For thee', he now says to Philoctetes,

> For thee the destiny is ordained that through these thy sufferings thou shouldst glorify thy life.

But you may say: is this not just the stubborn heart of man being corrected by the gods? Is the *Philoctetes* not just the best proof of what I am so ready to deny?

Let us suppose for a moment that we have all just returned from the siege of Troy and that I feel impelled to tell you what a good sort Philoctetes was to come along and finish off the weary business for us, especially after the rather shabby way we had treated him. But, you might well reply, who wouldn't have gone to Troy to be cured of so terrible an affliction and in addition to gain such glory from his exploits? Only a madman would have declined to go to Troy in such circumstances. To such an answer I could offer no reply, unless I could assure you that I had learnt from Neoptolemus and Ulysses themselves that even health and glory were not sufficient to tempt Philoctetes to help us—that it was Hercules himself who sent him, and that he could not deny Hercules only because he was bound to Hercules by ancient ties of purest loyalty and love. In short that Philoctetes joined us not for any material consideration, however worth while or much desired in itself, but only in obedience to the call of a loyalty that let him feel he was at last a free agent in a worthy service.

Hercules is the symbol of that freedom of the spirit that comes to those dedicated to a service to which their hearts can give no denial. Instead of being the tool of men, the slave of the Atreidae, Philoctetes is the companion and heir of Hercules. It is the service in which is perfect freedom. To say, as Mr. Ivor Brown suggests, that there is no free will in Greek tragedy is surely to ignore this paradox. At every stage Philoctetes chooses; at every stage his will is the deciding factor—he chooses as the artist himself chooses, and his will is finally identified with the service he accepts, as the will of the artist is identified with his art. We may call men like Bach or Beethoven or Rembrandt slaves of their Art if you like, or regard the man who trains to ride the Grand National on his own horse as a slave to sport, but only if we are so degenerate that we can do no more than envy and malign those who venture on those pinnacles and steeps of hardship on which we have turned our back. It is we who are the slaves and they who are the free men. And so it is in the tragedies of Sophocles—the protagonist you may call a slave to this or that, but his slavery proves on examination to be one of those passions or services that glorify men.

In the *Philoctetes* there is no support for those who insist that Sophocles is here concerned to discover for us the tragic flaw in some otherwise worthy character. It provides, however, an admirable proof of the force in Aristotle's answer to Plato's attack on the poets, and illustrates very clearly the variety of experience called *catharsis*.

The whole question of the acceptability to the moralist of such a figure as Philoctetes was reopened by Lessing in his review of some assertions by Winckelmann on the nature of Greek art. Winckelmann had insisted that the essential quality that gave ancient art its classic character was restraint. This quality of restraint he sought to illustrate in the marble group of Laocoon and his two sons. There the father, though himself in the embrace of the serpent and with his two sons entangled before his eyes, is not represented as shrieking aloud as in Virgil; the sculptor has indicated the father's agony only by showing his lips as parted sufficiently to allow the escape of some subdued exclamation. Here, said Winckelmann, the sculptor has obeyed the rule of classic decorum that forbids the unmanly exhibition of grief and pain. And in his enthusiasm for this classic restraint Winckelmann went on to compare the fortitude shown by Laocoon with that exhibited by Philoctetes in the play we have just been talking about.

Here Lessing intervenes; he was uneasy in reading that what Virgil permitted could be censured as unclassical. If Laocoon cried out in Virgil there must be good reason for it, Lessing felt. Further, if we are to talk of restraint in the *Philoctetes* it cannot be on the score that Philoctetes refrains from crying out. There is one episode that would be unduly brief were it not filled out with his cries and lamentations; the scene echoes with his loud and agonized appeals. How then can we talk of restraint and fortitude? Indeed, as Lessing pointed out, it was precisely this freedom of lamentation that had been criticized as unmanly by such different critics as Cicero and Adam Smith. Just as Plato demanded as models for his citizens calm and wise characters, unvarying in their constancy, so in the same spirit Cicero and Adam Smith censured the dramatist for choosing a character making such a display of his feelings and delivering so frontal an attack as it were on the sympathies of the audience. Here the critics felt was the indulgence in self-pity carried to excessive lengths.

Lessing's reply is characteristic of the great critic. True, Lessing agrees, Philoctetes cries out, but, he adds, it is not for nothing. The pain Philoctetes endures is sent by a god, a pain beyond mortal endurance. To his terrible physical affliction are added other heavy causes of grief—loneliness above all; these, however, Philoctetes endures with fortitude. And Philoctetes, when the chance does at last come to him of complete freedom from his overpowering torture, is not prepared to purchase such freedom with the loss of the freedom of his soul. The pain may conquer his body; it cannot subdue his spirit. The more terrible and agonizing the pain the greater the fortitude.

It is true then that Philoctetes might have been cited by Plato as an example of the lamenting hero. Lessing, however, has supplied the analysis that enables us to understand how Aristotle could answer this objection by drawing our attention to the *catharsis* of fear and pity effected by tragedy. The fear and pity are there as Plato complained, but there is something more: there is something that bears down before it like a deluge (to use Wordsworth's expression) every feeble sensation of disgust and aversion. What that something is Lessing has made clear. It is the determination in the hero to suffer and endure all things rather than submit to a thraldom that would employ his gifts in the service of deceit and selfishness.

In these final plays of Sophocles you can hardly refuse to see an explicit treatment of what Jaeger calls the Hellenic ideal of *areté*. Such men as Oedipus and Philoctetes have, to use the words of Heracles, glorified their lives through their sufferings. Reading back from these late to the earlier plays we can see that these too are embodiments of a vision inspired by this ideal. Sophocles is not inspired by any doctrine that comforts him with the notion that the gods destroy men or inflict on them an almost intolerable fate only for their faults. To justify Creon's treatment of Antigone or find in Deianeira's love for her husband some moral flaw is in the words of Philoctetes

To shelter behind the gods and make the gods liars.

Why men like Oedipus and Philoctetes should have to be glorified through suffering Sophocles does not profess to know, although many have pretended that he does make such a profession. What Sophocles does know is that they are glorified—it is in this glory he finds his inspiration, and to give form and body to this inspiration is the end of his art.

We have now looked at three authorities, shall we say, to whom the producer of the *Hamlet* film might appeal to justify his use of the lines

So, oft it chances in particular men . . .

as a Prologue and key to the drama. He might have referred us to Bradley or Aristotle or to Sophocles. All these insist or are said to insist on the centrality of the doctrine of *hamartia*; yet, when we come to examine them for ourselves, Bradley and Aristotle, although they do offer us an interpretation of tragedy based on such a doctrine, yet add such qualifications that we might insist that they provide at the same time its refutation. Indeed the variety of experience on which the whole effect of tragedy depends—*catharsis* to use Aristotle's term—does not rest on the faults but on the virtues of men. And turning to the Greek tragic artists themselves, we find they have been submitted to a form of interpretation that taken at its face value can end only in the denunciation of Sophocles we have had from Mr. Ivor Brown. On the premises he accepted Mr. Ivor Brown is justified; but the premises are not derived from the text of Sophocles, and Mr. Ivor Brown has denounced as a kind of conservative toady of the gods the man who stands with Shakespeare as the champion of what Milton called the high and heaven-born spirit of man.

Having rid myself, though not perhaps my hearers, of this prepossession that seems to bemuse all interpreters of tragedy that rely on it, I am now free to turn to look at Shakespeare's tragedies directly and not through this distorting medium. If I have not said enough so far to persuade you to abandon the ancient superstition, perhaps I may have done something to induce in you a willing suspension of disbelief for the moment, if you can bring yourself to listen to what I have yet to say on the inspiration and vision on which Shakespeare raised his tragedy.

# IV

## THE UNION OF OPPOSITES

IN the preceding stage of the argument, which was
to be regarded rather as a parenthesis, the contention was that the inspiration and very heart of Greek
tragedy was the dramatist's conception of *areté*. The
dramatist does not spare us what may stir fear and
pity to trouble our minds and even, as Keble felt
about the *Oedipus*, what may shock and appal us;
yet over against all this there is something in the
character and conduct of the protagonist that stands
out like the promontory, to use a favourite figure
with Sophocles himself, unmoved by the waves that
rage against it, the 'great sea-mark standing every
flaw' of Shakespeare's imagining to which one looks
for direction in the confusion of the storm.

Granted all this, for the moment, and even admit-
ting that Aristotle's insistence on the tragic *hamartia*
need not be taken too seriously, you may still say
that the main argument against the notion that
*Hamlet* is the tragedy of a man who could not make
up his mind has not been advanced at all, and that
for two reasons: in the first place it is generally held
that Greek drama and Elizabethan drama are very

different; and secondly, although these dramas are different, something was carried over through Latin channels from one to the other and the idea of the tragic flaw, while it may in Greek tragedy be considered for the moment *sub judice*, was emphatically the accepted doctrine of Shakespeare's day and may well be embodied in a type of tragedy that is different from, yet not entirely unrelated to, the Greek. The lines, therefore, beginning

So, oft it chances in particular men . . .

may indeed give expression to a doctrine familiar to Shakespeare and his audience and indicate the point of view from which the author wished us to survey the action.

Turning first to consider the view that there are certain fundamental differences between Attic and Shakespearian tragedy, we may take particular note of two differentiating factors the commentators have almost always been delighted to elaborate for our instruction. The Attic drama was, they tell us, religious. It certainly formed part of what had been a religious rite; the Chorus moved round the altar of Dionysus, and his priest sat in the very forefront of the audience; the plot of the tragedy usually centred on some mythical figure, and the connexion between the popular stories for tragedy and the cult of the hero's tomb was often implicit and could become explicit as in the *Oedipus at Colonus*. The Elizabethan drama, on the contrary, was purely secular we are told; religious topics were taboo; the Master of the Revels would not have countenanced any serious speculation by the dramatist on the mysteries of the Christian faith.

The second note of difference between the dramas that is dwelt on by commentators is consequent on the first. Greek tragedy was one manifestation of a long and all-embracing tradition; while the tragedies of Shakespeare, we are told, are devoid, or comparatively devoid, of all preconceptions. Shakespeare, as Lowes Dickinson contended in his *The Greek View of Life*, 'was free to choose what subject he liked and to treat it as he would; and no sense of obligation to religious or other points of view, no feelings for traditions descended from a sacred past and not lightly to be handled by those who were their trustees for the future, sobered or restrained for evil or for good his half-barbaric genius. He flung himself upon life with the irresponsible ardour of the discoverer of a new continent; shaped and reshaped it as he chose, carved from it now the cynicism of *Measure for Measure*, now the despair of Hamlet and of Lear, now the radiant magnanimity of *The Tempest*, and departed leaving behind him not a map or chart, but a series of incompatible landscapes. . . .

What Shakespeare gave, in short, was a many-sided representation of life; what the Greek dramatist gave was an interpretation.'

Summing up this contention we might say that the Greek dramatist is represented as religious and therefore as having a purpose in his dramas that is governed by his religious outlook: Shakespeare in comparison is purely secular and has no other purpose than to amuse or at least entertain the spectators 'by stimulating their emotions and no more', as Sir Maurice Bowra put it the other day, or, as Bridges put it long ago,

Shakespeare aim'd at exciting his audience to the limit of their endurance in the *Othello*, as he terrifies in the *Macbeth*, harrows in the *Lear*, and mystifies in the *Hamlet*.

Now if this contention had any real substance in it we should not be able to go on to regard Shakespeare as the expositor of some doctrine such as Bradley finds between his lines, nor should we be justified in using Aristotle's *hamartia* as a key to his dramas. For this is the very key with which those who insist on the religious character of the Greek drama unlock its purpose to us. Yet by hypothesis we may say the two dramas are different. If, in Greek drama,

the true tragic hero is a man of high place and birth who having a nature not ignoble has fallen into sin and pays in suffering the penalty of his act, if this is the Greek hero, what difference is there between him and the Shakespearian hero? How can we say the Greek hero is viewed religiously while the Shakespearian hero is not, unless we deny to Shakespeare any such doctrine as is supposed to permeate the Greek drama? Of course I am aware that some writers do not hesitate to say in one sentence that the two types of drama are worlds apart, and in the next sentence but one find in both as a central doctrine the conviction that all turns on some form of *hamartia*. But although we may find that in writing, we will, I trust, think again before we ourselves subscribe to it. You cannot at one and the same time hold that there is a fundamental difference between Greek and Shakespearian tragedy and that they are alike in the very core of their inspiration and conviction. There are obvious differences, but these are not fundamental if each has *hamartia* inscribed on its heart. You can say they are similar and both turn on the tragic flaw; or you can say they are different, and, since Shakespeare exploits the tragic flaw, the Greek dramatists must have worked on different lines.

Fortunately, you may reply, I have left you in no dilemma, for have I not argued that the Greek drama does not turn on any *hamartia*? You are free, therefore, to continue to affirm that the two types of drama

are very different and that Shakespeare adopted by
instinct or by study the traditional and current Aristotelian doctrine of the tragic flaw. We shall not argue
meantime with you, you may say, about the nature
of Greek drama; we shall suppose that we have all,
Aristotle included, been wrong on this particular point,
till the truth was disclosed by someone or other to you.
We still believe, however, that the Elizabethans were
in the same state as we were when in our unenlightened
condition, and that they shared with our yet uncon-
verted selves the idea that tragedy was built round
a fatal flaw in the hero. This, we hold, is the doctrine
as enunciated by Hamlet on the battlements.

You must add, of course, that you now reject
utterly the view of those who like Lowes Dickinson
represent Shakespeare as a semi-barbarian. You now
believe that Shakespeare had as clear and definite
a purpose as the Greek dramatist, although it may
have been different; for Lowes Dickinson must not
only have misunderstood the nature of the drama he
was commending to us so fervently, he was also mis-
informed about the historical background to Shakespeare's productions. It was possible for him when
he was writing in 1896 to regard Shakespeare's
audience as little better than a crowd of ignorant
toughs. Even in the *Encyclopaedia Britannica* of 1911
you can read over the initials of a very well-known

scholar that Shakespeare wrote for a dull-witted audience, that his drama is magnificent but incoherent, and a great deal more that the writer was subsequently taught to change his mind about. No wonder classical scholars, when they read the critics of Shakespeare with more attention than they give to Shakespeare himself, form so historically incorrect a portrait of Shakespeare as we find in the pages of Lowes Dickinson. Even in 1930 Mackail told us that Shakespeare was not 'in the modern sense of the term an educated man', that 'there is no evidence or likelihood that he was a great reader', and that 'It would be idle to look in Shakespeare for what is called good taste. His taste was pretty much that of his public.' It would be unkind to dwell on such misrepresentations were it not necessary to make clear to you how easy it was for so cultured and sensitive a scholar as Lowes Dickinson to talk nonsense about Shakespeare.

Shakespeare was working in a tradition, moral, political, and religious, that had developed round the Christian faith; he was appealing to a sense of values that needed doubtless the quickening touch of his words and symbols before his audience could follow him in his explorations, but theirs was far from an untaught sense of values. Shakespeare could not, even had he so wished, have drawn his characters and stories from the Bible, yet the Bible was better known, in the sense of being more familiar, in England in Shakespeare's day than in any other country in the world. As a recent study by a very distinguished American scholar has summarized the matter:

> Combine the message of the Gospels, the conception of 'laws and their several kinds' as codified in Hooker, the humane spirit of the circle of Colet, More, and Erasmus, and the moral emphasis of the Homilies, and one has the basic system of the popular drama in the time of Shakespeare.

And Professor Harbage does not hesitate to give the synthesis the label of Christian humanism. And he continues,

> Of primitive delight in action, combat, courage, and trickery there is ample evidence; but the heroes must conform with the system. Henry V must pray before battle, Robin Hood must forgive his enemies, and even Tamburlaine, cruel barbarian though he is, must preserve the chastity of Zenocrate and triumph only over those who merit the scourging of God. Citation must be highly selective, but inferences may be drawn on the extent of the commitment to Christian ethic by the response to its central and most difficult tenet. Freud has described the 'all-embracing love of others' as a modification of the sexual instinct, 'an impulse with an inhibited aim' (as rational an explanation as any), and has noted that such love is difficult, unreasonable, of questionable utility, and

indeed somewhat absurd. In 1562 the official homilist was coping with identical objections in 'Information of Certain Places in Scripture'. Citing Christ's bidding to turn the other cheek, and Paul's to feed one's enemies, he says, 'These sentences, good people, unto a natural man seem mere absurdities, contrary to all reason', and then patiently explains the nature of counsels of perfection.

It is in such a milieu that Shakespeare produces his plays. He knows, when he submits his characters from Plutarch or Saxo Grammaticus to the judgement of his hearers, the stops of his audience and the compass of their sympathies. Shakespeare had behind him the Middle Ages, and although he is in no way medieval, for to distinguish between right and wrong, good and bad, is not the difference that separates the Middle Ages from the other Ages of our civilization, he was able to develop a language that drew from that tradition, as say Sophocles did from his, a vital significance that did not seem alien or strange to the minds of his audience.

You may object that the dramatists and Shakespeare were speaking to the natural man—the audience were not in church; they were in the theatre and could relax from any moral rigidity they may have assumed in the Sunday pew. Yet there is a sense in which the theatre-goer is more exacting in his ethical standards than the church-goer. Even in men whose virtue, paralysed by self-interest, is unexercised, the sense of right and wrong exists, and when such a man finds himself in the theatre where his purely selfish interests can relax, even when he is reading a newspaper or a novel, that sense makes itself felt, and the heart however hardened towards the living becomes enlisted in fiction on behalf of the weak, the righteous, and the persecuted. We are all familiar with the paradox that disinterested and just conduct is by none exacted with more rigour than by those who are the most attentive to their own interests, or the most indulgent to their own passions. The comic artist excites our laughter at such an incongruity—he is the power with the gift that enables us to see ourselves as others see us without our knowing it. The tragic artist too can count on an audience composed of idealists in spite of themselves.

Poets, who have such an audience to deal with, must apply themselves to the moral constitution of the heart. The unconscious critical acumen, to use Trollope's phrase, of such an audience is both just and severe. The Elizabethan audience felt that Shakespeare applied himself more powerfully and consistently to principles they themselves perhaps could have formulated only in the most stereotyped and imperfect manner. Shakespeare naturally does not use the language of the pulpit; to do so would be to forgo the advantage and purchase the theatre gives over the minds of men, without acquiring the authority of the church. For the same reason he does not adopt the idiom of the rostrum, for the moral philosopher and the formal psychologist, however acceptable in the lecture room, demand from those who are to understand them a more elaborate form of matriculation than can be purchased at the theatre door. To attempt to reduce Shakespeare to an expositor of contemporary moralists is a further form of historical misunderstanding that may detain us for a few minutes.

The accepted view of tragedy, however, in the Elizabethan mind was Aristotelian, you may say. Those of that age who discuss the problems tragedy raises are, we are told, of this opinion, although there are exceptions. In her denunciation of Bradley as a renegade from the true hamartian doctrine, Professor Lily Campbell appealed to those she regards as the philosophers and psychologists of the Renaissance. Bradley's morality and psychology were both unscientific and unhistorical, she instructs us; we must turn to such profound thinkers as Timothy Bright on *Melancholy* or Thomas Newton on the *Complexions* if we are to understand Shakespeare.

For the poet was, she is convinced, a 'popular philosopher':

The poet was no true and just poet unless he knew the moral philosophy where men's moral natures were described. In all this criticism there is little suggestion that the artist look about him at living men to obtain his material. In fact the inductive method for artists had not yet been discovered. The artist took his characters from moral philosophy.

It seems to me you might as well say men's blood began to circulate only after Harvey had written his *De Motu Cordis*. Were I to ask you who invented the inductive method in poetry and who were the philosophers and psychologists to whom Homer gave his nights and days, you would decline to answer so rhetorical a question. You would not be betrayed into such absurdity.

No one has yet tried to interpret Shakespeare in terms of the theologians of the day, for when you look into them they are far from being in agreement, though talking presumably of the same subject. The philosophers are also divided, but many of them, according to Professor Campbell, came to the conclusion that if you had a fall you must have deserved it. They felt like Eliphaz the Temanite, Bildad the Shuhite, and Zophar the Naamathite, that only on some such supposition could they justify the ways of

God to men. Such philosophers were back in the land of Uz with Job's friends and without the excuse these three comforters had, for Job's friends had not the advantage of having read the *Book of Job* or they might have spoken more wisely, and charitably. The philosophers, however, have Professor Campbell's approval:

[Their philosophy] came to seek the justice which must inhere in such falls if there was a God of justice in his heaven. And it found that justice in the error or the folly which caused men to bring down evil on themselves. And gradually it came to find in men's passions the cause of their errors and their folly, and therefore the cause of the evil they bring upon themselves. Thus fortune is not to be dissociated from cause in the change from happiness to unhappiness. Hamlet tells us that fortune's star is not to be separated from that defect in a man's nature which makes it operative.

Shakespeare's heroes then are slaves of passion.

We may, however, be permitted to suspend judgement for the moment on a thesis that requires us to believe that Shakespeare took his views on men and their actions from the philosophers rather than from his own observation of his fellows and his knowledge of the world. To suppose that Shakespeare's characters can be reduced to a kind of puppet-show illustrative of the discourses of such writers as Timothy Bright or Thomas Newton is at best unsatisfactory. If the lesson to be taught by tragedy is no more than this, that we must balance passion by reason, we had better get it unadulterated by the prejudices of the poets and take it cold drawn from the treatises of the philosophers.

With this philosophy is associated the psychology of the day, and if those who ask us to believe that Shakespeare followed the philosophers, because poets had not yet learnt to use their own faculties of eye and ear and their powers of reflection, are demanding more from our credulity than it can give, the students of Elizabethan psychology are often no whit behind them in taxing our understandings. Miss Ruth Anderson published in 1927 a treatise on the subject of *Elizabethan Psychology and Shakespeare's Plays* and, as it has recently been recommended to us by an Oxford Scholar, it will not be unfair if we cite Miss Anderson's conclusion as representative of this line of historical inquiry.

Bradley you may remember was defective as a critic not only morally but psychologically. If Professor Campbell puts him right on the first topic, correction on the second comes from Miss Anderson, for it seems

Shakespeare thought with his contemporaries on subjects of mind and ethics. His psychology was a crude explanation of observable facts, based on the science of the Middle Ages and cultivated in its development by a desire to understand the functioning of the soul for the better regulation of conduct.]

The results, as you might expect, are not in accordance with the findings of modern psychology. We can therefore understand Shakespeare only if we study the ancient system. There are, it seems, inconsistencies in Shakespeare's work which are, however, consistent with Elizabethan psychology. Here is Miss Anderson's summing up:

Modern psychology finds unity in human behaviour; hence we have come to demand of our literary artists works that are well-knit in purpose and impeccable in characterization. We have also allowed ourselves to forget that Elizabethan thinking emphasizes variability and even inconsistency in conduct.

Shakespeare, accepting the view held by his contemporaries, could not have been greatly concerned with consistency in characterization. . . . Usually, moreover, he was handling old material, sometimes even old plays. His characters do the things previously set down for them to do, and this fact may account in part for their inconsistencies. Shakespeare was also making use of a theory which teaches that our lives are 'not all of a Piece, but made up of disagreeing and different Parcels'. Conflicting motives and contradictory actions could not have troubled him as they trouble us today. In the light of Elizabethan thinking, therefore, his characters are more rational beings than we have hitherto supposed. His plays in other respects, also, are richer in meaning.

Shakespeare's characters become more rational, it seems, when we consider them in a manner we now reject as irrational. Were we to argue this way in any other field we should, I fancy, be dismissed as muddle-headed. Suppose we agree that the old phlogiston theory of combustion is incompatible with that of oxygenation proposed by Lavoisier. We accept, shall we say, the latter view as the only tenable explanation of the phenomenon. Do you think the older theory becomes more rational because we can now see where its exponents were mistaken? Understanding the cause of error does not make the error right. Are we to believe that Shakespeare's characters seem acceptable and rational only when we consider them in the light of opinions we now regard as delusions? In Art, to borrow a remark from Tovey, 'nothing is true which a change of date can make false'. If the essence of Shakespeare's work lay in these outmoded speculations of the psychologists it would have lost its interest long ago. To attempt to establish the meaning or significance of Shakespeare's work by the line of argument used by Professor Campbell or Miss Anderson is to mistake the true historical approach to the work of art. Such interpretations preclude any historical understanding of Shakespeare's career as an artist and of his struggle to formulate in his work what he himself had learnt from his study of man and the actions of man.

Dismissing pseudo-historical methods of interpretation, you may now say, still leaves us with the contradictions these imperfect methods were designed to explain away. Will any historical method you approve of resolve these contradictions for us? As it is simplest to work with some concrete and typical instance before us I take what has seemed to many commentators an obvious contradiction in *Hamlet*, especially as the Oxford admirer of Miss Anderson has very recently proposed to resolve it for us on her method. Here is how Mr. Bamborough formulates his problem and here is the solution he offers us:

It seems most likely that when Shakespeare came to rewrite the old play of *Hamlet* he found his hero described as 'melancholy', with reference only to his grief at his father's death, and possibly also to his discontent at being supplanted as king by his uncle. Writing about the turn of the century, Shakespeare may well, perhaps not entirely of set purpose, have expanded this hint into a character sketch of the melancholy man as he was popularly understood at the time without being too careful to ensure that his new introspective and intellectual hero— at once poetic and philosophic, cynical and idealistic— fitted exactly into a framework for a young and princely revenger. Subsequent criticism has fastened on and exploited the discrepancies thus produced.

There is a tangle of suppositions here that it would test your patience to tease out. Instead therefore of asking what Shakespeare may have had in mind at the turn of the century, let us look at what he had been doing in tragedy up till that time, in the hope that this study of his work in its historical setting may provide us with some clue to what he was aiming at in *Hamlet*. We know that, if we were to arrange Rembrandt's self-portraits in chronological order round a gallery wall, we should see not merely the changes in the artist's physical features, we should follow the development of an art whose purpose we could see emerging as clearly as we should see the wrinkles time was writing more freely from year to year on its subject's brow. Let us suppose that Shakespeare's work is hung like such pictures before us and that we can view them not merely as isolated phenomena but as the stages of a great endeavour.

Shakespeare's first tragedy was *Titus Andronicus*. We need not waste time arguing about its authorship, for it belongs to a type of tragedy Shakespeare was to put aside or so to develop that it became a different kind. It is a revenge play linked in date and source of inspiration with Kyd's *Spanish Tragedy*. Even if Shakespeare had only a share in *Titus* it would still remain historically important as an illustration of what was popular when Shakespeare was still a novice. Although I am persuaded that Shakespeare was the sole author, nothing in my argument will depend on this; you are free to divide the drama between various hands as long as you admit that its attribution to Shakespeare by Meres and its inclusion in the First Folio require us to accept it as in part at least from Shakespeare's pen. For our present purpose it might be neglected were it not for two features that will reappear later in the maturer tragedies.

Perhaps the first feature can best be described in a remark by Professor Garrod: 'Shakespeare was unscholarly enough to like blood and thunder.' There is, however, one word here that calls for examination and I fancy modification in the light of our own experience. Commenting on the popularity of the modern detective novel and its successor in America the hard-boiled story Mr. Somerset Maugham has observed:

They will be mistaken if they ascribe it to the increase of literacy which has created a huge body of avid but uneducated readers, for the 'whodunit', they will have to admit, was read also by men of learning and women of taste. My explanation is simple. The detective writers have a story to tell and they tell it briefly. They must capture and hold the reader's attention and so must get into their story with dispatch. They must arouse curiosity, excite suspense and by the invention of incident maintain the reader's interest. They must enlist his sympathy for the right characters, and the ingenuity with which they do this is not the least of their accomplishments. Finally they must work up a satisfactory climax. They must in short follow the natural rules of story-telling that have been followed ever since some nimble-witted fellow told the story of Joseph in the tents of Israel.

It would be equally unhistorical to explain the Elizabethan revenge play as raw material to satisfy the hunger of a savage and blood-thirsty audience. There are corpses strewn across almost every other scene of *Titus*, you may observe. But I have heard Oxford, and not Cowley or the other suburbs, but Oxford of the dreaming spires, described as the home of lost corpses. Now one of the most successful of modern practitioners in this genre has provided a formula for the beginner in his first attempts: when in doubt have a man come through a door with a gun in his hand. It will not do to say as one German commentator has argued that *Titus Andronicus* must have been written by a butcher's boy so free is the author with blood. For the blood is not that of calves and sheep but drawn in part at least from Seneca. The incision and cutting betray the dexterity of the not unlearned hand. We must therefore modify

Professor Garrod's remark to read: Shakespeare had in his youth a scholarly taste for blood and thunder.

Nor will it do to say that Shakespeare must have written his part in' this tale of slaughter with his tongue in his cheek. You might as well say the same of Kyd. Old Hieronimo became something of a joke in Shakespeare's own day, as was Tamburlaine himself. The scourge of God was a favourite with ancient Pistol. But no one will say, I think, that Kyd and Marlowe were not in earnest. The nearest parallel in our own day is Sherlock Holmes. Conan Doyle could never have enthralled two generations of readers had he been guying them. To suppose that the revenge play was the work of a joker is to ignore the evidence of our own experience. This, I venture to observe, is elementary.

The second feature in *Titus Andronicus* I should like to note is the conduct of the protagonist. Titus is pictured to begin with as the representative of the ancient Roman virtues: a devoted servant in mind as in body of his country, one who spares neither himself nor his family in that service, one to whom the ancient loyalties are not only guides but imperious masters. This man's troubles could have come only on such a devoted head; and so inhuman are the devices employed against him that we can feel his revenge however terrible was made to fit the crime. Of Titus you can hardly use the lines

> So, oft it chances in particular men
> That for some vicious mole of nature in them,

unless you treat his over-nice regard for his duty as a great defect. And his story is presented with all the care for the conduct of the action that explains, to Mr. Maugham at least, the grip of the modern story of crime and retribution. Professor Hereward Price has dealt admirably with this aspect of the play in his lecture *Construction in Shakespeare*. Indeed so well constructed does he find the action of *Titus* that he thinks this feature alone is sufficient to mark the tragedy as Shakespeare's. It seems to me the completest representative of its kind: it out-Senecas Seneca and yet has the touch of Shakespeare.

Shakespeare's next tragedy is *Romeo and Juliet* and this takes us into the current of thought and artistic purpose that was to lead directly to the maturer tragedies.

Those who insist that some form of *hamartia* must be found as a central motif in tragedy have had considerable difficulty in accepting *Romeo and Juliet* as a tragedy at all. It is hard, however, to find any better description for a play in which two attractive and promising young people are cut off so prematurely—not to mention the other deaths that add their measure of woe to the main calamity. If that is not tragedy, what is? Yet great ingenuity is required by those who detect the tragic flaw in the characters. Hegel, who never lacked ingenuity, has observed that Romeo has the characteristic mark of the tragic hero (at once his greatness and his doom)—his complete identification of himself with the power that moves him—the onesidedness, as Bradley agrees, which the Cosmos insists on correcting with so savage a disregard for the devotion of the character; and Hegel would persuade us of the truth of his diagnosis by remarking that Romeo is not a son or a citizen as well as a lover; he is a lover pure and simple, and his love is the whole of him.

With this assertion by Hegel in mind let us pause to examine the central situation of the play, the scene on which the action turns. Here we see the two opposing feelings that constitute the idea of the play and give it its form; and we have been prepared for the force with which the hostile emotions will confront one another by the manner in which the confrontation is contrived. The opposing forces are given their completest incarnation in Romeo and Tybalt. In the opening scene that sets the stage for us, Romeo is dreaming of love, while Tybalt is raging round in his passion to keep alive a quarrel that has no meaning for him except the opportunity it affords of quarrelling. At the Capulet's dance both passions assume a greater reality; Romeo falls in love with Juliet, and Tybalt is prevented from falling on Romeo only by the intervention of old Capulet himself. Next day when Romeo and Tybalt confront each other in the presence of Mercutio and Benvolio it is clear we have at last reached a crisis; here the opposites are face to face, yet even at this point Shakespeare contrives to intensify the antagonism in the situation. Romeo ignores the affront put upon him in the presence of his most intimate friends by this insulting bully. It is to this phase of the action I should like to direct your thought, for such forbearance on the part of Romeo seems to me, in spite of Hegel's assertion, to mark him as a worthy citizen. To say that he is a good citizen because he is in love does not surely detract from his conduct.

Looking more narrowly at the episode we would agree, I suppose, that were Romeo afraid of Tybalt or a very self-regarding cautious sort of man we might say he did wisely without our admiring his discretion. But we very quickly learn that Romeo is a man who, when the occasion calls, knows no fear and has no self-regard. It is not fear then that makes him behave like a good and law-abiding citizen. But I have heard it objected that Romeo, while he maintains an admirable steadiness in this central episode and shows perfect discipline under fire as it were, does at other times, especially in the scene where he learns of his banishment, show a deplorable lack of self-control. What would Plato have thought of this young man who casts himself on the ground and is for doing away with himself, and all for a chit of a girl he had met only the evening before? Surely this is a deplorable example for Shakespeare to exhibit to his countrymen, and indeed, as it has happened, to the world in general. Surely Romeo is here the slave of his passion; and how are we to reconcile this with his conduct elsewhere, especially when he thinks all hope is gone and the depth of his despair is reflected only in the stillness of the surface of his behaviour? Does Shakespeare make his characters, as some have contended, just what seems to him most effective in any particular scene, regardless of the total impression we may take from the whole?

Those who argue on these lines are like Hegel, though for the opposite reason, blind to a fundamental principle that operates in art no less than in life. Hegel insists on the one-sided obsessional character of the tragic hero, the intense but narrow or restricted unity of his nature, while the other party insists on the uncoordinated and essentially contradictory state of the elements in his make-up.

Both views are, I judge, wrong, as the following considerations, if you admit their validity, prove.

The fundamental principle I refer to is put most tersely and simply by Pascal in the *Pensées*.

> I cannot admire the excess of any virtue, such as valour, if I do not see at the same time the excess of the opposite virtue—as in Epaminondas who had the extreme of courage and of humanity.

This is the famous passage in which Pascal goes on to insist that greatness is to be found not at one extreme but in touching two extremes so as to fill all the in-between. To this notion of the *entre-deux* Sainte Beuve has devoted a well-known chapter in his *Port Royal*. There he observes that when we know a distinguished man only by repute or at a distance as it were, when we see only his dominating features, we are sometimes surprised, on more intimate acquaintance, to find him so different on other sides from what we imagined and so complete a figure. Speaking of Saint François de Sales he calls him, in order to emphasize these apparently contradictory qualities, not a dove in gentleness but an eagle in gentleness, so powerfully yet graciously does de Sales transport the listener.

Pascal himself had in mind a passage in Montaigne's essay *Of Profit and Honesty* where the opposites in the genius of Epaminondas are illustrated:

his undaunted courage, his ever ready compassion; the great leader who judged that person a bad man, 'how good a citizen so ever, that amongst his enemies and in the fury of a battle spared not his friend or his host'.

Such opposites as are contemplated by Montaigne and Pascal are not contradictions in character, and Lessing has made admirable use of the idea of the *entre-deux* in his discussion of the apparently conflicting phases in the conduct of Philoctetes:

> The lamentations are those of a man, but the acts are those of a hero. Both compose the manly hero who is neither effeminate nor hardened, but at one time appears as the former, at another as the latter, even as nature, principle, and duty alternately require. It is the sublimest subject which wisdom can produce and Art imitate.

Lessing's words apply as forcibly to Shakespeare's treatment of Romeo as to the characterization of Philoctetes by Sophocles. The lamentations of Romeo may indeed be those of the lover but the acts are those of the hero; and his conduct is presented to us in varying lights even as nature, principle, and duty alternately require. Juliet had no need to feel ashamed of the passioning of a lover who never hesitated when he thought her dead to press after her into the grave itself.

Shakespeare is now obviously working on the

same basic principles as Sophocles. Just as the Greek dramatist draws out for us the various aspects of the character of his hero, so Shakespeare indicates the extremes between which his character moves that he may stand in our imagination not as a bundle of contradictions, nor as a one-sided obsessed being, but as one in whom the elements are so mingled that we can see even in the extremity in which he finds himself a whole man.

*Romeo and Juliet* is still in certain aspects immature, that is when compared with later tragedies; yet in it Shakespeare discovered the idea he was to develop so powerfully in his later work; and the form which the idea takes in *Romeo and Juliet* has many obvious parallels, as I hope we may later agree, in *Hamlet*. It is in the study of this development that the historical investigation of Shakespeare's work must find the clue that will guide us through the labyrinthine paths that research has constructed from the social or literary or linguistic facts of his Age. Without such a clue we shall be trapped in the maze and devoured by a misbegotten monster of our misguided enthusiasms.

Between *Romeo and Juliet* and *Hamlet* comes *Julius Caesar*. There is no need to dwell on the union of opposites that go to the character of Brutus. As he anticipates in his union of the philosopher and the

soldier the combination of scholar and soldier we
have in Hamlet, it will be sufficient to say here that
in *Julius Caesar* Shakespeare takes up again the
tragic idea where he left it in *Romeo and Juliet,* and
that when we come to *Hamlet* we shall not be surprised to find commentators diagnosing as contradictions and opposites those extremes which are
complementary in characters with any pretensions
to heroic stature. Instead of supposing that Shakespeare was now in *Hamlet* attempting a sketch of the
melancholy man as he was popularly understood
about 1600 and that the dramatist fitted this sketch
very imperfectly into an old story, so imperfectly
that criticism can exploit the discrepancies—instead
of making these assumptions, let us consider this
play in the light of the earlier tragedies, in the hope
that from the comparison we may arrive at observations on which conclusions may be safely built.

Between the central situation in *Hamlet* and that
in *Romeo and Juliet* there exists a number of obvious
parallels. In the first place Hamlet holds his hand
against his uncle as Romeo holds his against Tybalt,
but very soon after both strike the fatal blow that
drives them into exile, and they return only to the
final catastrophe.

In the situation in which Romeo finds himself
when confronted by Tybalt, he is not, as far as I

know, accused of cowardice by any of the commentators; and this although he might, from the first scene where he appears as a sort of mooning lovesick youth, and from his subsequent violent passion for Juliet, be regarded as too effeminate to fight. He actually so describes himself when he learns of Mercutio's death; yet no one takes him at his word; and this because subsequent events make it plain even to the most critical that it is neither fear nor some subtle complex that keeps his hand from his sword. Everyone can see that it is because he is plighted to Juliet and that he finds the world on that blazing July day so good that he would have it go well even with Tybalt.

Turning to Hamlet's conduct in the prayer-scene we find the considerations that seem to guide the judgement on Romeo's behaviour no longer in general operation. Hamlet is like Romeo to begin with lost in a kind of reverie, yet his later actions are no less decisive than Romeo's, and he is clearly a very formidable opposite. Why then do commentators almost unanimously reject the suggestion that Hamlet may spare his uncle for reasons that do him as much credit as Romeo's forbearance does him? We admire Romeo for his humane conduct; why do we insist that we cannot and must not admire Hamlet's? Romeo was not called upon to stab a defenceless man, nor had Hamlet a chance of meeting his uncle on fair terms. Romeo had indeed to be a man to decline Tybalt's challenge without losing our sympathy. But might not Hamlet also be sufficiently a man to refrain without loss of face from stabbing a villain in the back?

Those who answer this question in the negative almost invariably disregard the considerations that Montaigne or Pascal or Lessing raises about the complementary nature of apparent opposites in the characters of men. Here, for example, is how a learned commentator has recently answered the question:

> Though these [that is the compunctions that have been suggested as holding Hamlet's hand] are qualities commonly associated with today's men of fine moral fibre, they are not in themselves, not even now, a necessary adjunct of high morality; how, otherwise, would our war-heroes be fitted into a high moral system?

The commentator may, I am sure, be acquitted of the belief that a good soldier cannot be a man of high moral character. Yet he seems to say so. But surely a hero is not necessarily a man of coarse moral fibre; the happy warrior is obviously a man on the model of Epaminondas, as humane as he was courageous. Nor does the same scholar see that he is overlooking the vital critical point made by Lessing in his criticism of Philoctetes when he goes on to say that, since Hamlet has no squeamishness at the sight of blood, we cannot suppose he had any moral compunction about stabbing the kneeling king. Surely the point is that if Hamlet had had some fear of looking on blood his inaction would be mere weakness and no credit to him. It is just because Hamlet does not shrink from blood when it is proper to shed it that we can find a moral explanation of his hesitation here. Hamlet is like Romeo in this: it is not any lack of nerve that makes him decline to act.

Nor will it do to suggest that in Shakespeare's day such compunctions as we might attribute to Hamlet are quite unhistorical. Epaminondas lived nearly 2,000 years before Shakespeare, and if you reply that Europe had not yet reached the heights of humanity attained in ancient Greece, we must answer that Montaigne at least could understand such a character and the excellence of a man at once fearless and humane. We have no reason to suppose Shakespeare less perceptive. We can see his treatment of the *entre-deux* motif in *Romeo and Juliet* and in *Julius Caesar*; we can trace its further development in the later tragedies—why should we reject it as inadmissible in *Hamlet*? To do so is to reject the only relevant evidence, the works of Shakespeare viewed in their historical relationships; as well as to

arrogate to ourselves a refinement of feeling we
deny to individual Elizabethans.

Hamlet's conduct then in the prayer-scene is not
contradicted by his killing the eavesdropper in his
mother's closet or his dispatch of Rosencrantz and
Guildenstern to England with the altered instruc-
tions; any more than is Romeo's forbearance towards
Tybalt incompatible with the later fury. Hamlet's
victims, as he says himself, made love to their
employment, and we can see that his conduct in
these emergencies affects us otherwise than his
stabbing the king would do. It is not because we are
superstitious that we dislike the prospect of such a
blow. It is, no doubt, a scruple hard to measure in the
crude balance of reason, but so delicate is the poise
of the scales of art that such a scruple not merely
turns but weighs down the beam.

Hamlet indeed, as all the critics have insisted, is
shown us in a succession of contrasts; yet it is precisely by these apparent contrasts that the dramatist
secures the unified and dominating impression the
character leaves on us. Let me insist on this point
once again by a final illustration from the play itself
and a last comment on the principle that I am ventur-
ing to maintain is the secret of the wonderful variety
and no less wonderful unity of the piece.

Hamlet's conduct in the graveyard has given rise

to much moralizing and unfavourable comment. This is what too much thinking brings one to; or this is what comes of going to Wittenberg—is a not untypical observation. I should like you, however, to consider it in relation to his conduct on the battlements when he says to those who would keep him from the Ghost,

> I do not set my life at a pin's fee;
> And for my soul, what can it do to that,
> Being a thing immortal as itself?

and I should like you to use as a link the following passage in which the principle I am trying to enforce is so perfectly illustrated for us by Wordsworth:

Simonides, it is related, upon landing in a strange country, found the corse of an unknown person lying by the sea-side; he buried it, and was honoured throughout Greece for the piety of that act. Another ancient Philosopher, chancing to fix his eyes upon a dead body, regarded the same with slight, if not with contempt; saying, 'See the shell of the flown bird!' But it is not to be supposed that the moral and tender-hearted Simonides was incapable of the lofty movements of thought, to which that other Sage gave way at the moment while his soul was intent only upon the indestructible being; nor, on the other hand, that he, in whose sight a lifeless human body was of no more value than the worthless shell from which the living fowl had departed, would not, in a different mood of mind, have been affected by those earthly considerations which had incited the philosophic Poet to the performance of that pious duty. And with regard to this latter we may be assured that, if he had been destitute of the capability of communing with the more exalted thoughts that appertain to human nature, he would have cared no more for the corse of the stranger than for the dead body of a seal or porpoise which might have been cast up by the waves. We respect the corporeal frame of Man, not merely because it is the habitation of a rational, but of an immortal Soul. Each of these Sages was in sympathy with the best feelings of our nature; feelings which, though they seem opposite to each other, have another and a finer connexion than that of contrast.—It is a connexion formed through the subtle progress by which, both in the natural and the moral world, qualities pass insensibly into their contraries, and things revolve upon each other.

Holding Yorick's skull or confronting the Ghost, Hamlet is one and the same being; and elsewhere as here Shakespeare has secured a fundamental unity.

Nor need we insist that, because in *Hamlet* Shakespeare is using a familiar story as the basis of his plot, there must necessarily be discrepancies in his treatment of it. The Greek dramatists all handled familiar myths but their dramas are not necessarily full of contradictions. Each dramatist gave his characteristic turn to the story he worked on. Aeschylus, Sophocles, and Euripides each wrote a drama on the story of Philoctetes; although only that by Sophocles has survived, we have a report of the others, and it is clear how they differed as the personality of their creators differed. Each work no doubt might have illustrated some aspect of the history of the fifth century, but we should have found, above and beyond all that, the stamp of the creator's mind. It is this personal touch, the development of a peculiar power of organization, that must take first place in any historical study of an artist's work. Today we have considered, however briefly, some aspects of the development of the complexity of Shakespeare's characterization; in the next and final instalment of my argument I shall discuss the individual stamp he has placed on the story he has used as the material for his *Hamlet*.

# V

# THE COMPLETE MAN

HAVING argued, with the support of the testimonies that the great students of life and literature have left us, that the range of feeling found in the protagonist of a Sophocles or a Shakespeare, although it may touch what seem opposites, is, far from destroying the unity of the dramatist's conception, the surest evidence of a vital organizing idea that gives life and reality to the creation—having dwelt on this variety, I come now to the unity, to the idea of life that governs everything.

Before doing so, however, I should like to interpolate some brief remarks on one type of contradiction I have not discussed and that I must dismiss in summary fashion, and this in spite of the length to which some have gone in the treatment of the matter. In a well-known essay *The Influence of the Audience on Shakespeare* Robert Bridges maintained a thesis that has since been taken up and enlarged, and indeed so puffed out that for quite a number of years the notions there expressed almost passed as the orthodox doctrine for believers in Shakespeare. The strange thing about this cult was that those who adopted it should have bothered about Shakespeare at all; for the central tenet of their belief was that Shakespeare took advantage of his illiterate, rude, iron-nerved and thick-witted audience to pass off on them a series of plays that are constructed round what we can see is a palpable dishonesty or theatrical trick. Shakespeare, we are told, took some story of violence and crime and created for this plot a character in whose personality we become so absorbed that we fail to see that such a character could never have participated in the horrors of the original story:

F.N .

> In the original the actor would be known and judged by his actions; this Shakespeare reverses by introducing his hero as a man superior to his actions, his art being to create a kind of contrast between the two which has, of course, no existence in the original tale.

For examples of such treatment we are referred to *Macbeth* and *Othello*; and *Hamlet* too, according to Bridges, is but one more instance of Shakespeare's illusionist technique; for the critic asks

> Why has there been such question whether Hamlet was mad, unless it was Shakespeare's design to make and leave it doubtful? And does not the hypothesis of such a design reconcile all?

Such a hypothesis, however, fails to explain why the world goes on being interested in *Hamlet*, unless we are as ignorant and stupid as the first audiences that were taken in by Shakespeare's sleight-of-hand. Were we to take the hypothesis seriously we should have to exclude Shakespeare from our schools and universities as an arch-deceiver of mankind. Yet scholars have elaborated the doctrine and with such applause that one must suppose that many enjoy the intellectual fun of sawing off the branch they sit on from the trunk that supports it, for here their levity is exempt from the correction of the law of gravity.

There is no need to argue now on the larger issue, for I hope all I have to say contradicts their assumptions. My point today is that Shakespeare selects some particular story for a purpose—that purpose being the same type of purpose as moves any man entitled to the name of poet or dramatist. It is thoughtless to say that Shakespeare's purpose was merely to entertain his audience—there is entertainment in every form of art. Yet no one says as he examines the fugues of Bach that the master has chosen or treated his subjects in a manner that can be described as merely calculated to entertain his listeners; the explanation of the treatment must be found in the laws of the art and the genius of the composer. Shakespeare's Tragedies entertain generation after generation because they provide an analogous form of pleasure. This is how Wordsworth puts it:

The Poet writes under one restriction only, namely, that of giving immediate pleasure to a human Being possessed of that information which may be expected from him, not as a lawyer, a physician, a mariner, an astronomer, or a natural philosopher, but as a Man.

Nor let this necessity of producing immediate pleasure be considered as a degradation of the Poet's art. It is far otherwise. It is an acknowledgment of the beauty of the universe, an acknowledgement the more sincere because it is not formal, but indirect.

No one thinks of the strokes of a fine billiard player or of the shots of a good golfer as the result of their desire to please the public. They please the public only when they play the game well; they could not have acquired their skill had they spent their time wondering how to please. To say, as a man holes a stiff putt that draws applause, 'There he goes playing to the gallery again', would be to confess that you did not understand the game. To suppose that you can sit down and write *Hamlet* or *Lear* because you are thinking only of what will please your audience, or that all the wonderful strokes of imagination can be explained as but one more effort to catch the fancy of the spectator, is a strange doctrine to come from a poet, and that a poet of so fastidious a mind and so devoted to his art as was Bridges.

It is not, however, this monstrous delusion I wish to discuss, but only one aspect of the evidence used by Bridges to justify the whole tissue of his sophistry —namely, the contradictions between the material elements in the plot, which Bridges refused to regard as mere carelessness but took for the symptoms of a deeper defect in Shakespeare's art. So he argues:

> The only kind of carelessness which is possible [here] implies intention; a paradox which a simple illustration may elucidate. When, in *Twelfth Night*, Malvolio picks up Maria's letter, he says, 'By my life this is my lady's hand: these be her very c's, her u's, and her t's, and thus makes she her great p's.' Now in the superscription which he immediately reads, there is no c, nor any p, small or great.

What Bridges notes is true; but what Shakespeare wanted was the somewhat aged but timely jest suggested by the word cut. Sir Andrew comes over the letters again so that those in the audience who were as slow-witted as Sir Andrew is supposed to be might catch up. If you are so matter-of-fact that you think Shakespeare should have seen to it that all the letters were in the superscription, you should take up some other study than literature—some form of history or shall we say science. Such detail Shakespeare often ignores in his concern for the effect as a whole, and he expects you to have sufficient gumption to go with him in the business. In *Othello*, to take an outstanding example, it is so imperative that the audience feel for themselves that Othello's charge against Desdemona is utterly false—otherwise there would be some wiseacre to say we had only Desdemona's word for it, as a commentator has recently insisted that we have only Hamlet's word for the boarding of the pirate ship—that Shakespeare arranges his scheme so that infidelity of the kind in question is a physical impossibility. We can all understand how the situation in which Othello and Desdemona found themselves afforded a wonderful opportunity for slander and jealousy; what the audience must see is that the accusation is the invention of wickedness.

That type of contradiction then, the purely material kind, I do not discuss here. What I have been examining with you earlier are those contradictions that would, were they indeed contradictions, deprive the drama of all claim to be 'more philosophic and of graver import than History'. The statements of drama would not be the *universals* described by Aristotle. 'By a universal statement I mean', says Aristotle, 'one as to what such or such a kind of man will probably or necessarily say or do—which is the aim of poetry, though it affixes proper names to the characters.' Were Bridges right Shakespeare's universals would be the most bogus statements imaginable; they would not be worth examining, because they would be meaningless.

The discrepancy between plot and character, which Bridges finds 'intentional' in the sense that Shakespeare needed some such untruth with which to surprise his audience, seemed to Bridges inevitable on his assumption that 'from the constitution of things it is difficult to imagine a character or personality whose actions shall be at once consistent and surprising'. Yet the men who have made it their business to study the constitution of things judge otherwise. 'Life', says Mr. Somerset Maugham, 'is full of improbabilities which fiction does not admit of', and he is speaking of improbabilities of character and conduct. Fiction may indeed have to halt after reality, but it has generally been admitted that of all who follow life Shakespeare best keeps pace with it. Bridges ventures to suggest a more probable set of reactions for Macbeth than those given him by Shakespeare. If the critic's assumptions about the incompatibility of consistency and surprise were indeed true his conclusions would be acceptable. But his premise finds no sanction in the studies of those whom the world has regarded as the most profoundly read in our nature. As Wordsworth says,

The study of human nature suggests this awful truth, that, as in the trials to which life subjects us, sin and crime are apt to start from their very opposite qualities, so are there no limits to the hardening of the heart, and the perversion of the understanding to which they may carry their slaves.

Shakespeare in *Macbeth* has embodied for us a process that Wordsworth affirmed he had seen with his own eyes. When therefore we find a modern commentator like Professor Fluchère asserting that

there is no relation of cause and effect apparently between the terrible scene of Duncan's murder and Lady Macbeth's sleep-walking scene which comes years later,

we can only conclude that his study of a line of criticism to which Bridges gave the authority of his name has blinded yet one more disciple to the nature of Shakespeare's art and to the realities on which it rests. Lady Macbeth's case might have come straight from the pages of a textbook of psychiatry.

It was the discrepancy between plot and character that Mr. Bamborough fancied he found in *Hamlet* that provided the mark for our attention in the later stages of our examination of the play. The apparent contradictions he explained by assuming that they were the result of Shakespeare's attempt to fit a character study of a melancholy man as understood about 1600 into an old revenge story. To this we replied that what Mr. Bamborough took for contradictions we regarded as the surest evidence of the artistic unity of the play; and pointed out that Hamlet, as far as the character can be considered as an individual entity, was drawn on lines perfected by Sophocles in his *Philoctetes*, lines that Shakespeare himself was developing in *Romeo and Juliet* and *Julius Caesar*. Shakespeare was employing as an artist a technique that gave life to the *entre-deux* principle expounded by such critics as Pascal and Sainte-Beuve. The character who grieved in the graveyard over the evidence of man's mortality could, it was argued, follow without flinching the transformation of these poor remains into the base uses to which even Alexander's clay might come only because there was within him so strong a sense of the immortal part that wears the vestment of decay. We must now consider the character not as a separate entity but as a function of the idea that gives its form to the play, and ask if we find in the combination of character and plot a vital unifying purpose.

We may begin by putting aside all fanciful conjecture about the nature of the early version of *Hamlet*; that it was originally written by Kyd in two parts of five acts each and reworked by Chapman is an instance of a type of assertion that we need not concern ourselves with. That there was an early version of *Hamlet* we know; it must date from at least 1589; the first recorded performance was in 1594 when Shakespeare's company performed it with *Taming of a Shrew* and *Titus Andronicus* during their short season at Newington Butts. Some scholars think that Kyd was the author of this early version; others regard it as an early version by Shakespeare. Fortunately for our purpose there is no necessity to argue the matter here. What we have now to consider is this: given the story of Hamlet we find in Saxo Grammaticus and Belleforest, and given the play we know as *Hamlet*, can we see the purpose that prompted Shakespeare's treatment of the material? If we can with this material before us demonstrate the artistic unity of Shakespeare's creation, there will be no need to appeal to some unknown version to close a gap in the logic of Shakespeare's argument. If successful, we need not ask whether Mr. Bamborough's conjecture, that the early version presented a picture of a prince pining in melancholy for his father's death or because of his exclusion from the immediate succession to the throne, is supported by any trustworthy evidence. We shall be content to leave such hazardous reconstructions to others, for, however interesting such speculations may be, they are, if found unnecessary for the solution of our critical problem, of no immediate value.

In the earlier forms in which we find the history of Hamlet, it is in part a revenge story. Here is how Belleforest, with Saxo Grammaticus as his guide, describes Hamlet's action:

A man (to say the trueth) hardie, couragious, and worthy of eternall commendation, who arming himself with a crafty, dissembling, and strange shew of beeing distract out of his wits, under that pretence deceived the wise, pollitike, and craftie, thereby not onely preserving his life from the treasons and wicked practises of the tyrant, but (which is more) by a new and unexpected kind of punishment, revenged his father's death, many years after the act committed.

In his enthusiasm for such a man Belleforest goes on to expand Saxo's comment that:

By his skilful defence of himself, and strenuous revenge for his parent, Hamlet has left it doubtful whether we are to think more of his wit or his bravery;

for Belleforest himself says that Hamlet in

effecting his purposes with so great boldness and constancie, left a judgement to be decyded among men of wisdom, which was more commendable in him, his constancy or magnanimitie, or his wisdom in ordering his affaires, according to the premeditable determination he had conceaved.

Belleforest adds scriptural authority for such a vengeance as Hamlet took for his father. In short here is the complete revenge story including the feature admired by connoisseurs in that kind, the new and unexpected form of punishment the avenger visits on his victim.

When we compare the plot of *Hamlet* with the original story, it is difficult to think of an adaptation of an original that could retain and develop so much of the given material and at the same time transform it all so wonderfully as does the play.

Putting aside the assumed madness for later and more detailed examination, we may, like everyone else, note Shakespeare's retention of the three traps that Fengon in the original sets for Hamlet: first the fair and beautiful woman, now however the fair and innocent Ophelia; then the eavesdropper whom Hamlet kills in his mother's chamber and whose carcass he fed to the swine; finally the courtiers who accompany Hamlet to England. All these impersonal agents start into life at Shakespeare's touch and stand before us as Ophelia, Polonius, and Rosencrantz and Guildenstern, just as Hamlet's foster-brother becomes Horatio. Then there is the funeral that meets Hamlet on his return to Elsinore. In the original Hamlet arranges with his mother that she will celebrate his funerals a year after his departure for England; he returns himself to take part in them; in Shakespeare he returns to see the interment of Ophelia. Finally the exchange of swords in the duel with Laertes recalls the device by which Hamlet in the original story hands Fengon a useless weapon and dispatches the miscreant with his own sword. During the funeral celebrations the drinkers nail Hamlet's sword in its scabbard to save the prince as they fancy from his own folly. When the revellers are drunk and incapable Hamlet brings down the hangings on them, and pegs them fast with the crooks he had whittled as he sat in the ashes by the fire; having set the hall ablaze on the helpless drunkards Hamlet goes round to the bower where his uncle rests. Waking up his antagonist Hamlet ends this particular chapter of his story with the gesture that confirms his artistry in revenge.

The resemblances of structure between the original and the drama are something like the similarities that link the skeleton of a fish and that of *homo sapiens*: there are parallel features, but some parts are transformed almost beyond recognition. The analogy cannot be pressed, for Shakespeare has grafted on the original structure what might at first sight look like alien elements. The actors and the ghost come into the story from outside; nor could there be any scene in the original corresponding to that fixed at the very centre of Shakespeare's scheme. There could be no prayer-scene in Saxo or Belleforest, for there the King is at Hamlet's mercy only in the last minutes of their long duel: in Shakespeare the prince could have stabbed his uncle almost any day he wished. Finally, Shakespeare, having given up entirely the kind of tension provided by a revenge story, in which the avenger is waiting or searching for the weakness in his opponent's guard without exposing his own life, has also discarded the revenge finale that presents us with 'a new and unexpected kind of punishment'. If Hamlet were, as so many say, a revenge play it would score poorly compared with *The Spanish Tragedy* or *Titus Andronicus* for its conclusion. Indeed, so much of his original has Shakespeare forgone that it astonishes me that those critics who are so ready elsewhere to point out how Shakespeare has missed the real opportunities his material offered him have not here dwelt at more length on his ineptitude.

In *Hamlet* Shakespeare has, as it were, developed from the primitive genus a new type with a very different nervous system; he has transformed a cold-blooded into a warm-blooded creature. Yet just as a salmon say—since we are comparing the organization of fish and mammal—has its own type of excellence, so the original Hamlet-story has its characteristic merits that should not be over-looked.

We are apt to refer to the original Hamlet as a brutal avenger, a cunning but uncompunctious foe; but, as the quotations I have already made from Saxo and Belleforest prove, the earlier authors present the prince to us as an ideal type. He is a man of honour who will 'not tarnish the unblemished lustre of his fame by timidly skulking from his fate', nor will he purchase his life by any mean submission or even by falsehood; for, says Saxo,

He wished to be held a stranger to falsehood; and, accordingly, he mingled craft and candour in such wise that, though his words did not lack truth, yet there was nothing to betoken the truth and betray how far his keen-ness went.

The early Hamlet is, besides, a man of 'over great melancholy'; the author is here accounting for Hamlet's powers of divination. By 'melancholy' then is signified what *Melancholia* stands for in Dürer's famous and mysterious engraving. Melancholy gives the scientific and searching or the artistic and creative temperament. In Saxo we read how the King of England 'adored the wisdom of Hamlet and thought it were inspired'; for Hamlet had signalized his arrival at that monarch's court by a series of observations and deductions beside which the conclusions of Sherlock Holmes are elementary. With a more than Watson-like admiration the King, on verifying the statements that his bread and wine were tainted, that his wife was the daughter of a bondmaid, and he himself the son of a slave, insisted on giving this inspired guest his daughter to wife. In Shakespeare we sense the genius of the man; it is safe to say that there is no other character in fiction that so impresses us with this feeling. It must be noted, however, that 'melancholy' is not necessarily an impediment to action. The vehemence of Hamlet's melancholy in Belleforest or the power of his divination in Saxo in no way hinders the prince in his business of revenge; it is the gift that ensures his success.

In brief the original Hamlet is the ideal prince, as tough and resourceful and ingenious as you can conceive, the 'mark and glass' to an age that did not pull its punches. And Saxo offers us this judgement on Hamlet's life,

Had Fortune been as kind to him as Nature, he would have equalled the gods in glory, and surpassed the labours of Hercules by his deeds of prowess.

This encomium is expanded by Belleforest who, however, feels he must add one important qualification, a qualification demanded by the literary convention of Belleforest's own day. Hamlet is still the

perfect example of all the virtues 'if one only spotte
had not blemished and darkened a good part of his
praises'. Hamlet had, it seems, like Hercules and
Samson what is called a weakness for women. Hamlet is betrayed by his second wife—a Scottish
Princess I am sorry to have to say—and Belleforest
tells us how glad he is of this opportunity to enlarge
on the frailties of women. Hamlet, Saxo tells us, so
loved his wife 'that he was more deeply concerned
in his mind about her future widowhood than about
his own death, and cast about very zealously how
he could decide on some second husband for her
before the opening of the war', a war he did not
expect to survive. According to Belleforest Hamlet
might have spared himself his concern, for the lady
was very well able to take care of herself and with
the fickleness of her sex was quickly on with the new
love almost before the old lay dead. Saxo stresses
Hamlet's love for his wife—*charitate tenebatur*;
Belleforest insists that he was 'besotted on his wife'
—*celle qu'il idolatroit*—and Belleforest is happy to
honour not merely the literary convention of his day
that looked for the tragic flaw, but to point a moral
that I am sure he would have wished us by no means
to omit:

Thus you see that there is no promise or determination
of a woman, but that a very small discommoditie of

fortune mollifieth and altereth the same, and which time doeth not pervert; so that the misfortunes subject to a constant man shake and overthrowe the naturall slipperie loyaltie of the variable steppes of women, wholly without any faithful assurance of love, or true unfained constancy.

The Hamlet story in Saxo and Belleforest, whatever the intermediate stages may have done, presents the reader with a type of human perfection. Belleforest's little postscript about woman is merely an attempt to find in Hamlet's devotion to his wife the flaw convention had begun to require in the tragic hero. To Saxo the husband's devotion was a virtue even if misplaced, for Saxo does not himself have a high opinion of women's faith. Hamlet's is a perfection in keeping with the circumstances of the times in which he lived. Hamlet was an example to men in a world where no quarter need be asked, and Hamlet neither expected nor begged it. He is a worthy son of his famous hard-fighting father.

It is this relation between father and son, hardly touched on in the original, that Shakespeare has so wonderfully developed in the first act of his play. A network of relations, and the awareness that goes with this more complicated and integrated system, are created before our eyes. This is the nervous system as it were which provides the possibility of a new and more developed form of perfection, if on the heels of one generation a fresh perfection may tread. In Shakespeare, as we suggested earlier, Hamlet's father belongs to the heroic age; he inhabits the world in which Saxo places his son. When we come to Shakespeare, Hamlet has had time to study at Wittenberg; he belongs to a later world, but his task is not lighter than his father's. Where his father had wrestled with flesh and blood, the son has now an adversary of a more metaphysical and spectral kind. He must still carry the sword but he knows it may well be a sword that will not save.

Not a few commentators have dwelt on this meeting of the ages that provides the idea on which the play is built. Some do not hesitate to find in the encounter the central confusion in a play that seems compounded of contradictions. Shakespeare, they feel, has not played fair; he has put his civilized man into a prehistorical setting. You will find in the correspondence of Grimm and Diderot and their friends how just before the French Revolution these enlightened men felt that *Hamlet*, for it had been introduced as we saw to the French stage, was already antiquated. As one of them asks:

Why this continual repetition of great crimes in our theatrical representations and in a country where the petty manners are so far from the energy such crimes demand?

Yet the crimes in *Hamlet* are kid-gloved affairs compared with the monstrous deeds that were about to be enacted in the Revolution and in the name of humanity and justice. The delusion of the *philosophes*, however, is always with us, for in our own day Mr. Middleton Murry will have it that

The Ghost belongs to an order of existences, and his injunction to an order of morality, which have been left behind in the slow advance of humanity.

It does credit, doubtless, to the sentiments of men that their wish should be father to such a thought; but to indulge such sentiments at the expense of our intelligence leads not merely to a weakening of our aesthetic judgement and an inability to understand *Hamlet*, it leads to horrors such as Belsen. Our present business, however, is with Literature or with what aspires to that distinction, and I must ask you not to overlook in our academic abstraction the testimony of the bookstalls, and railway compartments, and even of the senior common-rooms of our universities, for there is displayed, absorbed, and created a type of fiction that has certain important features in common with the Elizabethan drama and with what may be called the tougher strands in *Hamlet* itself.

When the English detective story was first in vogue it was a luxury to be enjoyed by those comfortably ensconced behind the safety curtain of the British Navy and of a police force sufficient for the modest requirements of the criminal community. Since those days the world has become a much more dangerous place, at least for the inhabitants of this blessed plot called England. The classic detective story is giving place to a more realistic treatment of crime and murder, and it is natural perhaps that the American imagination, quickened by so up-to-date a phenomenon as Murder Incorporated, should have taken the lead and evolved the hard-boiled crime story. The corpses are no longer found in scented bath-water or amidst the fragrance of the magnolia blossom, and we may well ask ourselves what the justification is of the loss of the old amenities. Is this just another instance of that coming down in the world that we are witnessing in so many spheres political and social?

Whatever your feeling about it, I think we may agree it is an awakening to certain realities we should like to forget, if forgetting would abolish them. The readers as well as the writers of these stories, a distinguished practitioner in the genre surmises, no longer

believe that murder will out and justice will be done—unless some very determined individual makes it his business to see that justice is done. The stories were about the men that made that happen.

And, continues Mr. Raymond Chandler in *The Simple Art of Murder*:

The realist in murder writes of a world in which gangsters can rule nations and almost rule cities, in which hotels and apartment houses and celebrated restaurants are owned by men who made their money out of brothels, in which a screen star can be the finger man for a mob, and the nice man down the hall is a boss of the numbers racket; a world where a judge with a cellar full of bootleg liquor can send a man to jail for having a pint in his pocket, where the mayor of your town may have condoned murder as an instrument of money-making, where no man can walk down a dark street in safety because law and order are things we talk about but refrain from practising; a world where you may witness a hold-up in broad daylight and see who did it, but you will fade quickly back into the crowd rather than tell anyone, because the hold-up men may have friends with long guns, or the police may not like your testimony, and in any case the shyster for the defence will be allowed to abuse and vilify you in open court, before a jury of selected morons, without any but the most perfunctory interference from a political judge.

We need not allow ourselves to succumb to what we may call the Northanger Abbey complex and expect to find finger men or a boss of the numbers racket even at a lecture on Shakespeare. We can, for the moment, safely relax. But to say that the conditions described by Mr. Chandler do not affect us is to bury your head in the sand or to ignore the chance of its being buried for you by the rubble from a bomb. London is still scarred all over with the wounds it took in the recent gun duel with the greatest racketeers the world has so far known. The command of armies and fleets although it may give the pomp of circumstance to cold-blooded crime cannot, or should not, disguise from us its nature. It is not, however, the social and national danger in ignoring Mr. Chandler's survey that I wish to stress, but the danger of misunderstanding Shakespeare, if we are too short-sighted to see the background against which justice in this world has to be done. For in his Elsinore Shakespeare has created for us in manageable dramatic form the conditions that offer a challenge to the man whose business it is to see that justice is done. I turn back for a moment, therefore, to the new Elsinore of the modern crime story to ask what kind of man it is that makes it his business to see that what is wrong is, as far as nature and circumstances permit, put right. Perhaps we may return to Shakespeare with a better idea of his purpose in *Hamlet*.

Can we find anywhere an acceptable opinion about what may be called the ideal governing the hard-boiled story? Do any of its practitioners give us an inkling (apart from the example their work provides) of what they require of their hero? Here again I must turn to Mr. Chandler; 'In everything that can be called art', he says, 'there is a quality of redemption.' I must pause here and ask you to observe that we have now come upon another instance of a writer describing the phenomenon Aristotle called *catharsis*. Like Keats and Wordsworth, Mr. Chandler was probably not thinking of Aristotle and was making for himself a discovery Aristotle made for criticism generally over two thousand years ago. Mr. Chandler may, however, be deeply read in his Aristotle, and this possibility ruled out his observations from the earlier discussion, although I permitted myself the use of his term 'redemption'. Whatever the exact relation of Mr. Chandler and Aristotle the modern writer places the experience he calls 'redemption' as centrally in his reflections on his art as did Aristotle *catharsis* in his observations on tragedy:

In everything that can be called art there is a quality of redemption. It may be pure tragedy, if it is high tragedy, and it may be pity and irony, and it may be the raucous laughter of the strong man. But down these mean streets a man must go who is not himself mean, who is neither tarnished nor afraid. The detective in this kind of story must be such a man. He is the hero, he is everything. He must be a complete man and a common man and yet an unusual man. He must be, to use a rather weathered phrase, a man of honour, by instinct, by inevitability, without thought of it, and certainly without saying it. He must be the best man in his world and a good enough man for any world. I do not care much about his private life; he is neither a eunuch nor a satyr; I think he might seduce a duchess and I am quite sure he would not spoil a virgin; if he is a man of honour in one thing, he is that in all things.

He is a lonely man and his pride is that you will treat him as a proud man or be very sorry you ever saw him. He talks as the man of his age talks, that is, with rude wit, a lively sense of the grotesque, a disgust for sham, and a contempt for pettiness.

The story is this man's adventure in search of a hidden truth, and it would be no adventure if it did not happen to a man fit for adventure. He has a range of awareness that startles you. . . .

If there were enough like him, I think the world would be a very safe place to live in, and yet not too dull to be worth living in. *and we are.*

Did time permit I should like to enter a demurrer on behalf of duchesses and then draw out the similarities between Chandler's hero and Hamlet. Unfortunately, there are still a number of topics that must somehow be fumbled up into however loose a conclusion, and I can take the comparison only a little way, but far enough, I hope, to persuade you to take it farther. 'He talks as the man of his age talks, that is, with rude wit, a lively sense of the grotesque, a disgust for sham, and a contempt for pettiness' as

Hamlet does to Rosencrantz and Guildenstern, to
the grave-diggers, to Osric. 'He has a range of
awareness that startles you' as does Hamlet in his
soliloquies or with the actors or Horatio. 'He must
be a man of honour . . . and certainly without saying
it'—and it is one of the stumbling-blocks that critics
fall over when they argue that Hamlet cannot be
a man of honour because so far is he from claiming
to be so that he regularly represents himself as a
rogue or peasant slave or a coward or a brute. And
I need not add that those who failed to treat Hamlet
as a proud man would be sorry, if they could still be
sorry for themselves, that they ever saw him.

I am not equating *Hamlet* with the modern crime
story, but suggesting that if you are looking for a line
in tough-story making you will find it well marked
out for you by Mr. Chandler. As Shakespeare and
his contemporaries also favoured at times this type
of plot, we may not unprofitably compare the old and
new technique. *Hamlet* is much more complicated
than the modern crime story; as Mr. Maugham
observes, the modern author tells us little about his
hero's antecedents—'he seems to have neither
father, mother, uncles, aunts, brothers or sisters.'
Shakespeare fills in this gap: we know Hamlet's
university, and he has father, mother, and uncle, all
intimately involved in his story. If we imagine

Sherlock Holmes with a mother married to Professor Moriarty, the Professor, after finishing his famous Treatise on the Binomial Theorem, having included, while still holding down his Chair of Mathematics, Holmes's father among his victims, and Holmes himself writing love-letters to the daughter of Moriarty's senior lecturer, we may form some notion of the technical dexterity such additions would have required of the author. Shakespeare, however, in *Hamlet* did not need to stress the detection of the criminal, as Kyd did in *The Spanish Tragedy*, and he himself in his *Titus Andronicus*; he was free, as is the author of the modern hard-boiled novel, to concentrate on giving his hero character and personality; and has so triumphed over the complexity of his material that Hamlet is even to the simple-minded as living as Sherlock Holmes.

At this stage in what I call the argument, it is now possible to examine one element common to the original story and to the drama, with the hope of placing it in a truer perspective than that in which historical critics tend to represent it. In the original story Hamlet pretends to be a moron, so that his uncle may overlook the necessity of liquidating him and thus allow time for the counter-measures Hamlet has in mind. 'This cunning course', says Saxo, 'not only concealed his intelligence but ensured his safety.' Sitting by the fire, raking in the embers with his hands, Hamlet is fashioning the crooks that provide at one and the same time evidence of his folly and a weapon of his revenge. Belleforest decorates Saxo's version of this phase in the hero's behaviour by likening him to Brutus, who expelled the Tarquins; and David, Solomon's father, is also cited as an authority for so dissembling a policy. Even in the original story Hamlet's conduct did not entirely dispose of his uncle's fears, hence the various tests set by the King to try the real nature of his nephew's mind. In Shakespeare's drama Hamlet has no need of any protective covering. The King is only too ready to let bygones be bygones provided he has peace to enjoy the present. Hamlet's donning a coat of folly so far from making him inconspicuous only draws all eyes towards him and provokes the King's suspicions. The question of course suggests itself: Why should Hamlet deliberately adopt a pose that can only make his task more hazardous?

This question the commentators often answer by supposing that Shakespeare took over mechanically from his original a feature that was there an essential part of the machinery of the story. No madness, no Hamlet, would have been true in the situation described by Saxo. It is not so in Shakespeare, but the dramatist had to retain the situations in which

Hamlet is tried by his uncle; to find an excuse for them Shakespeare, it is maintained, adopted the old device, although it had now no satisfactory place in the economy of the plot. Shakespeare is able doubtless to exploit the distraction theatrically, but this is felt merely to deepen the impression that the dramatist has been more attentive to theatrical effect than dramatic truth.

In reconsidering the question, we are not bound to suppose that Shakespeare in using a traditional feature in his material put it to the same use as the original. The new context and new dramatic purpose make a new handling inevitable, if there is to be true unity of action. In the typical revenge story we have a character who does all in his power to induce in his intended victim a complete sense of security. Belleforest has explained the accepted technique:

He (the avenger) must speak and do all things whatsoever that are pleasing and acceptable to him whom hee meaneth to deceive, practise his actions, and esteeme him above all men, cleane contrarie to his owne intent and meaning; for that is rightly to playe and counterfeit the foole when a man is constrained to dissemble and kisse his hand, whome in heart hee could wishe an hundred foote depth under the earth, so hee mighte never see him more, if it were not a thing wholly to bee disliked in a christian.

Belleforest might be describing to us the tactics

of Montresor in Poe's revenge story *The Cask of Amontillado*, where the proper procedure is set out with Poe's mathematical precision. Here the avenger's obsequious attentions shepherd Fortunato into the cellar-pen where he is to die by inches. Nothing could be more abhorrent to Hamlet than such tactics. His uncle may cover his villainy with smiles, but such hypocrisy offends Hamlet almost more than the villainy itself. Hamlet's victim must know what is coming to him. Hamlet cannot tell the King in so many words what to prepare for, although he does this as near as need be in the nunnery-scene when he suspects that the King is listening; but Hamlet can create a thundery atmosphere that threatens a stormy sequel. Naturally he cannot insult the King openly unless the court feel there is some excuse; this excuse that keeps the matter between the King and himself his assumption of strangeness provides; the sting in his blunt remarks is for the King's private ear. Hamlet will not come on his victim silently and suddenly from behind; the final encounter must be face to face. All this is in keeping with his holding his hand against the villain at prayer. The antic behaviour is all of a piece with his conduct throughout; we have no need to create contradictions by confusing Shakespeare's creation with his original matter. If we read *Hamlet* as a self-contained work we can understand why Hamlet assumes the coat of folly.

To all this you may reply that, if you doubted Hamlet's sanity before, you are inclined to conclude from my interpretation that he was doubly mad. Why, you may ask, should an avenger behave in so out-of-the-way a fashion? Why can't he behave like an ordinary, sensible man, or why can't we suppose he should, and explain the bits and pieces that don't fit such a common-sense view as just stuck in to produce theatrical effects that would please the audience? I can only reply that if you choose to look at a work of art in that way, I won't try to dissuade you. Your line of approach dispenses with the labour of thought, and you can without effort have it as you like it. If, however, you are really interested in seeing any artistic creation as a whole, you must be prepared to have what you call your common sense disturbed from time to time. As a London scientist said the other day, as he explained some of the new ideas to the public: 'This statement has that touch of offending common sense which is the hallmark of every truly important scientific discovery.' It is regularly so in the world of art; the trouble is that unless you are very quick in that particular uptake you may find it hard to decide whether a new form of expression is indeed genuine or merely humbug. In *Hamlet*

Shakespeare has taken very special pains to prepare us for the discovery that what may be called the common-sense view of Hamlet's doings is quite inadequate if we are to understand his conduct.

Acting and soldiering may be said to be normal everyday activities, yet by the time Hamlet has commented on the performance of the First Player or on the business of the soldiers of Fortinbras we can see that to the eye of common sense there is a kind of madness in their ongoings. 'Don't do owt for nowt' may seem excellent sense, but to hold the sky suspended or save the sum of things for a shilling a day is a form of madness that is expected of soldiers, and we approve their conduct, for we know very well that man does not live by common sense alone but by the exercise of that *areté*, that virtue, whether it be that of the actor, or soldier, or the protagonist himself. All this Diotima long ago explained to Socrates when she told him that if he examined the doings of men he would find their aspirations utterly unreasonable, unless he understood what she was teaching him about the immortal *areté* all men long for, and long for the more the worthier they be. Shakespeare in the interludes with the actors or soldiers brings home to us the truth of what Mr. Chandler would say when he calls his hero 'a common man and yet an unusual man'. By 'common'

Mr. Chandler does not intend to say 'mean' or unworthy of our attention, for every man worth his salt is an unusual man and repays our regard. He uses 'common' in the sense by which we may identify Hamlet first with the actor and then with the soldier in their response to life. If these men are mad then Hamlet is doubly or trebly so. But if it is otherwise, then Hamlet is unusual only in the intensity with which he responds to things. In him is concentrated the vital drive he recognizes in humanity, and his denial to himself of the virtue he feels in common men only serves to confirm our sense that he himself is a complete man.

Tragedy, Shakespeare had come to see when he was writing *Hamlet*, is a kind of consecration of the common elements of man's moral life. Shakespeare introduces the common man in Hamlet not for what we are apt to think of as his 'commonness' but for this strange power however you care to name it that he possesses—we have used *areté*, or virtue, or we might have borrowed from Henry James 'the individual vision of decency'. In Tragedy there is no longer a Chorus moving round the altar of a god; but if Proust is right the spectators are still participants in a supernatural ceremony.

Perhaps I may put the aspect of Tragedy I wish to keep before you more clearly by drawing on

Professor Harbage's study of Shakespeare's ideal man. Collecting the approving references he finds that this ideal man is soldierly, scholarly, and honest. If these men seem to lack the larger idealism that is so common and abundant in our own generation, there is no suspicion that Shakespeare's men will fail to back with their own skin their apparently modest programmes. As Professor Harbage says: 'All soldierly, scholarly, honest men are potential martyrs'—you can substitute for 'martyrs' tragic figures. Of that Shakespearian type Hamlet is the ideal. Shakespeare had before him in Saxo and Belleforest what was presented as an ideal type. This type Shakespeare transformed. To what may be called *the instinctive wisdom of antiquity and her heroic passions*, represented so impressively by Hamlet's father, Shakespeare has united *the meditative wisdom of later ages* in Hamlet himself. There is no surrender of the old pieties, and the idea of the drama comes from the impact of new circumstances upon the old forms of feeling and estimation; there is a conflict between new exigencies and old pieties, that have somehow to be reconciled. The play dramatizes the perpetual struggle to which all civilization that is genuine is doomed. To live up to its own ideals it has to place itself at a disadvantage with the cunning and treacherous. The problem Mr. Chandler sets his hero is infinitely complicated in *Hamlet*—to be humane without loss of toughness. The hero must touch both extremes: without one he is just brutal, lacking the other he is merely wet. The problem Mr. Chandler has posed for the writer of the story of crime Shakespeare solved, I am suggesting to you, just after his thirty-fifth year, when he finally transformed the ancient saga-like story preserved for us by Saxo into the play we know as *Hamlet*.

# INDEX OF NAMES AND TITLES

Aeschylus, 91, 149.
*Ajax*, 87.
Anderson, Professor Ruth, 128–30.
*Apologia*, Newman's, 102.
*Apple Cart*, Shaw's, 23.
Aristotle, 38–39, 41, 45–47, 50, 57–65, 70–74, 78–92, 109, 111, 113, 115, 118, 120, 156, 174.

Bach, J. Sebastian, 3–5, 8, 108, 153.
Bamborough, J. B., 128, 131, 158–60.
B.B.C., 3, 48–49.
Beethoven, Ludwig van, 1, 108.
Belleforest, François de, 160–8, 178–9.
Benchettrit, Paul, 16 n.
Berkeley, George, 2.
Birrell, Augustine, 11.
Bowra, Sir Maurice, 118.
Bradley, Professor A. C., 39, 48–57, 61, 77–84, 113, 125, 128, 137.
Bridges, Robert, 118, 151–8.
Bright, Timothy, 125, 127.
Brohan, Augustine, 16.
Brown, Ivor, 93–97, 108, 113–14.
Burbage, Richard, 3.
Burke, Edmund, 12–13.
Butcher, Professor S. H., 58–61.

Campbell, Professor Lily B., 53–56, 61, 87, 125–30.
Casals, Pablo, 2–5.
*Cask of Amontillado*, 180.
Chandler, Raymond, 172–6, 182–5.
Chapman, George, 159.
Cicero, 110–11.
Coleridge, S. T., 64, 70.

*Complexions, Touchstone of*, 125.
*Construction in Shakespeare*, 136.

Da Ponte, 4.
Davenant, Sir William, 7, 11.
David, King, 178.
*De Motu Cordis*, 126.
Dent, Alan, vi, vii, 19.
De Quincey, Thomas, 64.
Dickinson, G. Lowes, 117, 120–1.
Diderot, Denis, 169.
Diotima, 182.
Dixon, W. Macneile, v, vi, 50.
Doyle, Sir A. Conan, 135.
Dryden, John, 7, 11.
Ducis, J. François, 9–10.
Dumas, Alexandre (père), 16.
Dürer, Albrecht, 165.

*Elizabethan Psychology and Shakespeare's Plays*, 128.
*Encyclopaedia Britannica*, 120.
Epaminondas, 140, 145–6.
*Ethics, Nicomachean*, 80, 90.
Euripides, 149.

*Figaro*, Mozart's, 4.
Fluchère, Professor H., 158.
Forster, E. M., 93.
François de Sales, St., 140.
Freud, Sigmund, 64–65, 74–76.

Galen, 67.
Garrick, David, 6, 9–17.
Garrod, Professor H. W., 133, 135.
*Ghosts*, Ibsen's, 27.
Godwin, William, 68–69.
Goethe, Johann Wolfgang, 31–34.
Granville-Barker, Harley, 1, 3–4, 28.

*Greek View of Life*, 117.
Green, T. H., 54.
Grimm, Baron, 169.

Harbage, Professor Alfred, 122, 184.
Harvey, William, 126.
Hegel, G. W. Friedrich, 50, 52–55, 137–9.
Heminge and Condell, 4, 8, 17.
Hermeias, 85–89.
Hicks, R. D., 59.
Holmes, Sherlock, 135, 166, 177.
Homer, 73, 81, 89, 95, 126.
Housman, A. E., 73.
Hume, David, 14–15.
*Hyperion*, 72.

Ibsen, Henrik, 27.
*Idiot Boy, The*, 68, 70–71.
*Influence of the Audience on Shakespeare*, 151.

Jaeger, Professor Werner, 81, 89, 91.
James, Henry, 31, 35, 183.
*Job, Book of*, 101–3, 127.
Johnson, Samuel, 9, 14.

Keats, John, 64, 66–67, 71–76, 83, 89, 174.
Keble, John, 94–97.
Kyd, Thomas, 132, 135, 159–60.

La Place, Pierre Antoine de, 10.
Lavoisier, A. Laurent, 130.
Lessing, Gotthold E., 72, 109–12, 141, 145.
*Lyrical Ballads*, 67, 73.

Mackail, J. W., 121.
Marlowe, Christopher, 135.
Maugham, W. Somerset, 24, 133, 136, 157, 176.
*Melancholia*, Dürer's, 165.

*Melancholie, Treatise of*, 125.
Meres, Francis, 133.
Meurice, Paul, 16.
Milton, John, 65–66, 114.
Montaigne, Seigneur de, 140–1, 145–6.
Morgann, Maurice, 48–49.
Mozart, Wolfgang A. C., 4.
Murray, Professor Sir Gilbert, 58.
Murry, J. Middleton, 170.

Nettleship, R. L., 54.
Newman, Cardinal, 95, 102.
Newton, Thomas, 125, 127.
North, Christopher, *see* Wilson, John.

*Observer*, 93.
*Oedipus at Colonus*, 97, 100–4, 117.
*Oedipus Tyrannus*, 91–92, 95–97, 103, 115.
Olivier, Sir Laurence, v, 18.

Pascal, Blaise, 45, 140–1, 145, 159.
Pericles, 74.
*Philoctetes*, 104, 107–10, 159.
Plato, 57, 73, 80–89, 109–14, 125–30, 139.
Plutarch, 123.
Poe, Edgar Allan, 180.
*Poetics*, 41, 57, 59, 60, 62, 72, 80–87.
*Politics*, 59.
Pope, Alexander, 11.
*Port Royal*, 140.
Price, Professor Hereward T., 136.
*Prolegomena to Ethics*, 54.
Proust, Marcel, 183.

Raleigh, Professor Sir Walter, 49.
Rembrandt, 108.
*Republic*, 108, 132.

Sainte-Beuve, C. A., 140, 159.

*Samson Agonistes*, 65.
Saxo Grammaticus, 123, 160–9, 177–8.
Seneca, 134.
Shakespeare, William: *Julius Caesar*, 142–3, 146, 159; *King Lear*, 8–9, 72, 94, 97, 118, 154; *Macbeth*, 7–8, 25, 118, 152, 158; *Measure for Measure*, 117; *Othello*, 118, 152, 156; *Romeo and Juliet*, 8–9, 136, 142–3, 146, 159; *Taming of the Shrew*, 160; *Tempest*, 7–8, 11, 117; *Titus Andronicus*, 132, 134–6, 160, 164, 177; *Troilus and Cressida*, 11; *Twelfth Night*, 155.
Shaw, George Bernard, 23.
*Simon Lee*, 68–69.
Simpson, R. R., 29.
Smith, Adam, 110–11.
Socrates, 84, 182.
Sophocles, 87, 91–97, 100–4, 109, 112–15, 123, 141–2, 149–51.

*Sophocles*, 91.
*Spanish Tragedy*, 132, 164, 177.
Steevens, George, 14.
Stewart, J. I. M., 29.

Tacitus, 52–53.
Talma, F. Joseph, 10.
Tate, Nahum, 8–9.
Tovey, Sir Donald, 130.
*Tragedy*, 50.
Trilling, Professor Lionel, 30, 74–75.
Trollope, Anthony, 124.

Virgil, 110.

Whitman, Professor Cedric H., 91.
*Wilhelm Meister*, 32.
Wilson, John, 69–70, 72.
Winckelmann, J. Joachim, 109–11.
Wolfit, Donald, 91, 93.
Wordsworth, William, 64–76, 83, 89, 112, 148, 154, 157–8, 174.

PRINTED IN GREAT BRITAIN
AT THE UNIVERSITY PRESS, OXFORD
BY VIVIAN RIDLER
PRINTER TO THE UNIVERSITY

N

MA

I